1981

THE GREEK TRAGEDY
IN NEW TRANSLATIONS

GENERAL EDITOR   William Arrowsmith

EURIPIDES: Alcestis

EURIPIDES
Alcestis

Translated by
WILLIAM ARROWSMITH

OXFORD UNIVERSITY PRESS
New York and London
1974

Printed in the United States of America

To my Mother and Father

EDITOR'S FOREWORD

The Greek Tragedy in New Translations is based on the conviction that poets like Aeschylus, Sophocles, and Euripides can only be properly rendered by translators who are themselves poets. Scholars may, it is true, produce useful and perceptive versions. But our most urgent present need is for a re-creation of these plays—as though they had been written, freshly and greatly, by masters fully at home in the English of our own times. Unless the translator is a poet, his original is likely to reach us in crippled form: deprived of the power and pertinence it must have if it is to speak to us of what is permanent in the Greek. But poetry is not enough; the translator must obviously know what he is doing, or he is bound to do it badly. Clearly, few contemporary poets possess enough Greek to undertake the complex and formidable task of transplanting a Greek play without also "colonializing" it or stripping it of its deep cultural difference, its remoteness from us. And that means depriving the play of that crucial otherness of Greek experience—a quality no less valuable to us than its closeness. Collaboration between scholar and poet is therefore the essential operating principle of the series. In fortunate cases scholar and poet co-exist; elsewhere we have teamed able poets and scholars in an effort to supply, through affinity and intimate collaboration, the necessary combination of skills.

An effort has been made to provide the general reader or student with first-rate critical introductions, clear expositions of translators' principles, commentary on difficult passages, ample stage directions, and glossaries of mythical and geographical terms encountered in the plays. Our purpose throughout has been to make the reading of the plays as vivid as possible. But our poets have constantly tried to remember that they were translating *plays*—plays meant to be produced, in language that actors could speak, naturally and with dignity. The poetry aims at being *dramatic* poetry and realizing itself in words and actions that are both speakable and playable.

Finally, the reader should perhaps be aware that no pains have been spared in order that the "minor" plays should be translated as carefully and brilliantly as the acknowledged masterpieces. For the Greek Tragedy in New Translations aims to be, in the fullest sense, *new*. If we need vigorous new poetic versions, we also need to see the plays with fresh eyes, to reassess the plays *for ourselves*, in terms of our own needs. This means translations that liberate us from the canons of an earlier age because the translators have recognized, and discovered, in often neglected works, the perceptions and wisdom that make these works ours and necessary to us.

A NOTE ON THE SERIES FORMAT

If only for the illusion of coherence, a series of thirty-three Greek plays requires a consistent format. Different translators, each with his individual voice, cannot possibly develop the sense of a single coherent style for each of the three tragedians; nor even the illusion that, despite their differences, the tragedians share a common set of conventions and a generic, or period, style. But they can at least share a common approach to orthography and a common vocabulary of conventions.

1. *Spelling of Greek Names*
Adherence to the old convention whereby Greek names were first Latinized before being housed in English is gradually disappearing. We are now clearly moving away from Latinization and toward precise transliteration. The break with tradition may be regrettable, but there is much to be said for hearing and seeing Greek names as though they were both *Greek* and *new*, instead of Roman or neo-classical importations. We cannot of course see them as wholly new. For better or worse certain names and myths are too deeply rooted in our literature and thought to be dislodged. To speak of "Helene" and "Hekabe" would be no less pedantic and absurd than to write "Aischylos" or "Platon" or "Thoukydides." There are of course borderline cases.

"Jocasta" (as opposed to "Iokaste") is not a major mythical figure in her own right; her familiarity in her Latin form is a function of the fame of Sophocles' play as the tragedy *par excellence*. And as tourists we go to Delphi, not Delphoi. The precisely transliterated form may be pedantically "right," but the pedantry goes against the grain of cultural habit and actual usage.

As a general rule, we have therefore adopted a "mixed" orthography according to the principles suggested above. When a name has been firmly housed in English (admittedly the question of domestication is often moot), the traditional spelling has been kept. Otherwise names have been transliterated. Throughout the series the -os termination of masculine names has been adopted, and Greek diphthongs (as in Iphigeneia) have normally been retained. We cannot expect complete agreement from readers (or from translators, for that matter) about borderline cases. But we want at least to make the operative principle clear: to walk a narrow line between orthographical extremes in the hope of keeping what should not, if possible, be lost; and refreshing, in however tenuous a way, the specific sound and name-boundedness of Greek experience.

2. Stage directions

The ancient manuscripts of the Greek plays do not supply stage directions (though the ancient commentators often provide information relevant to staging, delivery, "blocking," etc.). Hence stage directions must be inferred from words and situations and our knowledge of Greek theatrical conventions. At best this is a ticklish and uncertain procedure. But it is surely preferable that good stage directions should be provided by the translator than that the reader should be left to his own devices in visualizing action, gesture, and spectacle. Obviously the directions supplied should be both spare and defensible. Ancient tragedy was austere and "distanced" by means of masks, which means that the reader must not expect the detailed intimacy ("He shrugs and turns wearily away," "She speaks with deliberate slowness, as though to emphasize the point," etc.) which characterizes stage directions in modern naturalistic drama. Because Greek drama is highly rhetorical and stylized, the translator knows that his words must do the real work of inflection and nuance. Therefore every effort has been made to supply the visual and tonal sense required by a given scene and the reader's (or actor's) putative unfamiliarity with the ancient conventions.

3. Numbering of lines

For the convenience of the reader who may wish to check the English against the Greek text or vice versa, the lines have been numbered according to both the Greek text and the translation. The lines of the English translation have been numbered in multiples of ten, and these numbers have been set in the right-hand margin. The (inclusive) Greek numeration will be found bracketed at the top of the page. The reader will doubtless note that in many plays the English lines outnumber the Greek, but he should not therefore conclude that the translator has been unduly prolix. In most cases the reason is simply that the translator has adopted the free-flowing norms of modern Anglo-American prosody, with its brief, breath- and emphasis-determined lines, and its habit of indicating cadence and caesuras by line length and setting rather than by conventional punctuation. Other translators have preferred four-beat or five-beat lines, and in these cases Greek and English numerations will tend to converge.

4. Notes and Glossary

In addition to the Introduction, each play has been supplemented by Notes (identified by the line numbers of the translation) and a Glossary. The Notes are meant to supply information which the translators deem important to the interpretation of a passage; they also afford the translator an opportunity to justify what he has done. The Glossary is intended to spare the reader the trouble of going elsewhere to look up mythical or geographical terms. The entries are not meant to be comprehensive; when a fuller explanation is needed, it will be found in the Notes.

ABOUT THE TRANSLATION

The Greekless reader, if not the professional scholar, should perhaps be reminded that this translation is meant to be an accurate, but not slavishly accurate, rendering of the original. It is, I would like to think, an effort of truly liberal translation. That is, I have tried to translate according to the principle laid down by St. Jerome, that we should render according to the sense rather than the letter. My aim has been to realize, as best I could, the *dramatic* movement and unfolding poetry of the play; to follow, persistently but unobtrusively, in the most forceful and graceful English I could muster, the arc of feeling as it rises and falls, the growing pressures of action-inflected meaning in a complex structure. Admittedly, my notion of the play's "sense" is firmly—perhaps too firmly for those who would prefer the roominess of a more open structure—embedded in the translation. Here and there, and especially in the choral lyrics, I have been unashamedly interpretive, sometimes expanding metaphors and even intruding glosses where I thought them necessary. But my departures from the text have been deliberate, not absent-minded; and the reader who is willing to peruse the Notes in detail will find, in most cases, an explanation, if not always a systematic defence of my practice.

Lincoln, Vermont   William Arrowsmith

CONTENTS

ALCESTIS

INTRODUCTION

I

By general agreement the *Alcestis* is a spirited, puzzling, profound, and seriously light-hearted tragicomedy of human existence. But it is also, as I hope to show,[1] a peculiarly beautiful and coherent example of what, for want of a better word, I would call "modal" drama (as opposed to modern "psychological" drama or the drama of our own "theater of character"). Moreover, the beauty and the difficulty of the play—its mysterious elusiveness, its puzzling texture and unfamiliar form—can only be understood, I think, by grasping, in all its complicated richness, its peculiar thought and structure.

Among extant Greek plays, there is literally nothing like it.[2] For works of similar tone and structure, we must go to the late Shakespearean "comedies," to *The Winter's Tale* or *Pericles* or *The Tempest*; or, in music, to Mozart's *Marriage of Figaro*, with its miraculous blend of wit, pathos, and farce, its *buffo* Figaro and its semi-tragic Countess Almaviva. In composition, the *Alcestis* is remarkably executed; each succeeding scene unerringly articulates and inflects the controlling theme; even for Euripides (one of the most severely economical of dramatists, despite the censures of his critics), the concentration is extraordinary. So too is the shaping of the characters, each one, in his

---

1. For obvious reasons nothing more than a sketch is possible here. Demonstration and defense of what, in its aim and complexity, purports to be a coherent theory of Greek drama would require much lengthier treatment—in fact, a book. But a sketch, tentative and incomplete, may conceivably serve the reader's purpose (if not the scholar's requirements).

2. Presumably because it occupied, when first performed in 438 B.C., the position of a "satyr-play"; that is, rounded off a group of three tragedies. But since we know very little of "satyr-drama" (Euripides' *Cyclops* and a fragment of Sophocles' *Searchers* are the only extant examples of the genre—a quite insufficient sample), and the *Alcestis* is our only example of a "pro-satyric" play, it is impossible to describe or even identify the "genre."

generically revealing way, embodying or at least illuminating the central idea—the process by which a man, instructed by the example of a woman's love and courage, at last comes into his own humanity, into his true human mode, and finally learns, through suffering, humiliation, and luck, to think recognizably "human (that is, *mortal*) thoughts." It is an extraordinary achievement. But that achievement cannot, I think, be properly understood unless the play is seen and experienced in the modal terms that control its structure, tone, characters, and themes. The play is complex, but its complexity is organically coherent; superbly unified even in its mercurial shifts of pace and feeling, in its crisscrossed paradox and irony, it is all of a piece. What makes it so, I believe, is mode and modal concentration.

II

By "mode" I mean simply the generic states and phases of human (and other) existence, as they revealed themselves to the Greek mind and imagination. No ancient writer, of course, anywhere speaks of "modes" nor is there any ancient Greek word for "mode." But it is a revealing modern notion that primitive cultures are "primitive" precisely to the degree that they are typically incapable of articulating assumptions that lie deeply ingrained in language and behavior. But this seems a dubious notion at best since the more coherent the culture is, the less perceptible its basic assumptions are likely to be to members of that culture.

Modern scholars of Greek drama have constantly pointed out that ancient tragedy aims at the archetypal and universal, and their grounds for so doing are, in essence, modal. Indeed "modal" analysis is really nothing more than an effort to work out, in ramifying detail, the dramatic and cultural implications of this "universalizing" tendency of Greek drama. It implies not only that ancient drama should not, and cannot, be understood in terms of modern ideas of character and psychology, but that the very aim of Greek drama is an account of human fate in a world where any order of "being" is defined by contrast with other modes of existence. Also implied is the corollary that modal aims will inevitably be trivialized by imposing modern notions. Thus, in sharp contrast to modern drama, the drama of the Greeks is *masked*; its characters make their appearances in ways which quite literally compel the audience to perceive and respond to them in a generic, not an individual, way. Further, the modal aim of ancient drama is reinforced, as we would surely expect, by the theatrical and rhetorical conventions of that theater.

A few examples. In both Greek and English the distinction between "mortal" (*thnētos*) and "immortal" (*athanatos*) is a modal distinction rooted in language. Men die by definition whereas gods qua immortals cannot die; their modes differ according to their subjection to, or exemption from, death. Man is modally unique, and his uniqueness is explicitly revealed by informing contrast with the gods (who live forever and know it) and the animals (who are mortal but are unaware of their mortality). Men suffer necessity (*anankē*) whether as death, political oppression, old age, suffering, sexuality, or slavery; the gods who impose, and often incarnate, human necessities seldom suffer them. In short, the modes of men and gods are defined by their vulnerability to *anankē* or limits generally. Necessity is the criterion which divides each "species" of existence from the other.

But between man and man there are also crucial differences of modal degree, since men differ in their powers and therefore in their value. There are slaves, peasants, nobles, and free men; cowards, men of courage, and heroes. The hero is always interesting to the Greek mind because he is a modal frontiersman; he confounds old modalities and redefines the boundaries between man and god. One thinks of Herakles and his superhuman labors, Asklepios with his partial conquest of death, Orpheus with his harrowing of Hades—or the bravery of Alcestis. Or perhaps an Achilles, the archetypal *youth* confronted with the necessity of an early death. Implicit, often explicit, everywhere in Greek literature is a great hierarchy of being which runs from absolute, untrammeled Olympian possibility at the top, to sheer, wretched subjection to total necessity at the bottom. To this hierarchy the Greeks thought it possible and natural—indeed, almost second nature—to assign men and events. No body of thought is so overwhelmingly pervaded by such emphasis upon modal distinctions; no other literature is so concentrated upon the effort, to clarify, realize, and "place" the modes of existence. The spectrum is, of course, usually aristocratic, but the aristocracy involved is basically not that of blood but of achievement and *aretē*.[3]

This uniquely Greek concentration on the modalities has been slighted simply because it is so overwhelmingly obvious that the temp-

---

3. In range and suggestions, *aretē* is badly cramped by the prim English word "virtue." Originally, *aretē* designated something like Latin *virtus*, i.e. "manliness" or "physical prowess." Later it became the (quite untranslatable) term indicating the chief aristocratic virtues, ranging from "physical courage" to "excellence" to "moral courage"—that is, the qualities exhibited by an "excellent" man. Women might perhaps lay claim to *aretē*, but the word is essentially reserved to men. Euripides, in sharp contrast, stresses moral courage as against conventional aristocratic virtue, and clearly includes women among its rightful claimants.

tation is strong to dismiss it as cultural rhetoric or mere linguistic habit. This would be a mistake. For it is this modal obsession, this passion for observing the modes of men and gods, that gives Greek thought and art their characteristic coherence and clarity. Any object seems always to imply another. Individuals and details alike have a cosmic resonance. Unless one has a sense for modal composition it is, I think, very difficult to understand Greek literature. Needless to say, possession of a modal sense does not mean that the Greeks were amateur philosophers; they were rather the enthusiastic heirs of a fairly coherent culture whose values were, until the late fifth century, exceptionally coherent. Everything in their environment conspired to make them modally aware. The ordinary Greek surely had no more notion that he habitually made modal distinctions than Molière's *bourgeois gentilhomme* realized that he had been speaking prose all his life. But their audience's sensitivity to modes seems to have been assumed by Greek artists and dramatists, and their works are addressed directly to that understanding, as even a cursory examination makes clear.

→ Man (*thnētos*) and god (*athanatos*) are modal words, as I pointed out before. Similarly, the real force of the Delphic command to "know oneself" is modal. It means not that introspective awareness of identity and motives which moderns call "knowledge," but rather a recognition of one's place in the scheme of things: what it is to be a man, to possess a man's fate. The man who "knows himself" always knows one thing—his mortality. It is because he knows he is doomed that he will, in theory, act compassionately toward other men no less doomed than he. For this reason he avoids the dangerous adjectives, the epithets which belong to the gods—that blessed exemption from necessity that makes the Greek gods "happy," "immortal" (and also amoral). Because the gods see everything *sub specie aeternitatis*, that perspective of theirs obliterates both meaning and morality; since they do not suffer (or do so only rarely), they are seldom compassionate (that is, "fellow sufferers"). Man, who views things temporally, is defined as a transient and a suffering being; necessity for him is a way of life. Therefore, if he recognizes his fate, he will think "mortal thoughts" (*ta thnēta phronein*), and these thoughts will invariably be the facts of his condition: his fatedness, his limits, his death, even his Aphrodite. What man is not, god is: a concentration of supreme power and intensity, and in this sense god imposes man's necessity upon him. If a man is wise and thinks mortal thoughts, he will yield to god; only a great hero, a great fool, a great criminal, or a very young man (that is, a man who does not know himself because of his youth) will resist god. Why? Because he is contemptuous of the modes (like a man of *hybris*), or ignorant of them (like a young man whose *hybris* is natural), or defiant of them (like a hero), or innocent of them (like Admetos).

Everywhere in Greek literature the modes are implied in a structure of events, as the metaphysical basis of character, or as the given morality of the situation. Most Greek art—certainly Homer, Pindar, Herodotos, Aeschylus, Sophocles, and Euripides—is sustained modal meditation. The structure is often exactly designed so as to emphasize and intensify the modal distinctions between the characters; and just as the characters are defined in their own modes, so their modal differences define each other. Sophocles, for instance, constantly returns to stark, revealing contrasts between the hero (a person always ignorant of his modalities) and the *sophron* (or man of *sophrosynē*, the man who knows who he is). This, after all, is the difference between Oedipus and Kreon in the *Oedipus Rex*; between Chrysothemis and Elektra; between Antigone and Ismene; between Ajax and Odysseus. The pairing of these fated foils is addressed directly to an audience that feels situations modally. I stress *feeling* here because it seems important to realize that modal distinctions run deep. The Greek dramatist is not a philosopher, but a thinking artist whose sense of composition resembles that of his audience; modal perception, modal composition, are second nature.

Modal distinction, then, implies a hierarchy of value and being. The hierarchy differs, of course, according to the artist; each poet uses the same perceptual tools, makes similar modal distinctions, but inflects them in an individual way. But the work of art requires the reader to respond by placing men and events in an ordered relationship, each defining the other. The great modal example in Greek literature is, of course, Homer; all the others are variations on that great original. At the very top is god, sheer power, intense being; the quality "possessed by what is wonderful and unique," the special radiance of the exceptional and prodigious. Thus in the *Iliad* unusual men and great events have a luminousness which declares their divinity; it is because they are exceptional that they are divine. Among their many other functions, Homer's gods are often functional descriptions of the modes of great men; a hero is a hero, not because he enjoys the favor of a god but because his *aretē* requires a god's presence to account for it. The *aretē* reveals divinity, almost summoning the gods. Achilles' courage is like Odysseus' mother-wit and Paris' looks, a *charisma*. Every power a being possesses is pertinent to his place along this great gamut of being, running from the omnipotence of Zeus to the undifferentiated powers of the great feudal barons of Olympos, down to the modest particularisms of the nymphs and lesser powers, to the god-aspiring *aretē* of the hero, to the routine world of ordinary mortals, to weak women, helpless children, and chattel slaves. Each order suffers the cumulative *anankē* of the orders above it in an ascending curve of freedom and power. The hierarchy changes, needless to say, with the social period; Euripides' Athens is not Homer's Troy. In this flexible hierarchy, the man of *hybris* is dangerous not only to himself and others but to the order whose stability his *hybris* threatens. Against *hybris* the saving attitude is *sophrosynē*, which is little more than a mastery of the modes, a skill of acceptance and self-knowledge according to who one is, his powers and circumstances, according to his mortality. Some possess that skill; some do not. Most learn it naturally, but great men, men of exceptional good fortune, learn it the hard way because their greatness dislikes learning a limit.

In sum, necessity is the essential criterion of mode. For just as men are, as a species, differentiated from the gods by the *anankē* of death, so they are generically distinguished from each other by status, wealth, sex, and age. Perhaps the most obvious fact of the Greek masking convention is that it enables the audience to detect, at a glance, the generic traits of a character at the same time that it prevents his full individuation. His whole character, in fact, is little more than the sum of the possibilities contained in his "modal" presentation. We observe, for instance, that Euripides' Pentheus is a *boy*; but he is also a *king*; these two salient facts then combine to produce a third, his spiritual intransigence and pathetic susceptibility to Dionysos; and these "traits" are then given depth by contrast with old Teiresias and Kadmos. Hippolytos' defiant arrogance is a function not only of divine affinity—his indenture to the goddess Artemis—but of his youth, a youth sharply contrasted to the humble old age of the Huntsman. In the Greek theater, these defining traits are starkly visual; in most cases they are stressed by contrast and foil. The mask states the essentials, tells us whether its wearer is young or old or middle-aged; youth or young man; girl or matron; slave or free; prosperous or unfortunate.[4] These impressions are

4. For instance, according to our best authority on ancient masks, the lexicographer Pollux, a sallow (as opposed to a white) mask indicated that its wearer was "unfortunate or in love." See note on page 97. Not all scholars, of course, believe that Pollux' account accurately represents fifth-century practice. But T. B. L. Webster has, in my opinion, made a convincing case and my remarks are based upon acceptance of his argument. Those interested should consult Webster's *Greek Theatre Production*, pp. 35-73, and his "Notes on Pollux' List of Tragic Masks" in *Fetschrift für Andreas Rumpf*, pp. 141-50.

then amplified and "thickened" by language, plot, development of theme, and theatrical "blocking." But the essential lines by which a character is first introduced are never disturbed or distorted by intrusion of idiosyncratic detail. It does not follow in the least that the psychology of the modal character is therefore wooden or "stereotyped." Metaphysical or modal psychology may be unfamiliar, but it is no less rich and complex than any modern "individual" psychology.

The *language* of mode, the reader should note, is unmistakably and for obvious reasons the language of *anankē*. Indeed, one of the strongest arguments for a modal interpretation of Greek literature is the astonishing coherence of the abundant idioms and vocabulary of necessity. Thus we everywhere have expressions of force and strength; persistent verbal images of pressure or constraint or binding, the well-developed vocabulary of authority, coercion, deference, and obligation. There are also the metaphors and symbols, often visual, of yoking, wrestling, etc. If the reader is attentive to these nuances of force (and if the translator does not obscure them), his attention will be drawn not only to the situations which such language naturally applies but to the theme which language and situation together develop. This saturation (no other word will quite do) of Greek tragedy (but also epic, lyric, and history) in the idiom of necessity and force is, in my judgment, the single most obvious (but quite unexplored) fact of Greek tragedy.

The language becomes more impressive if the reader keeps the presumable "blocking" constantly in mind. "Blocking"—that is, the way in which the characters move in theatrical space, in relation to each other —has received far too little scrutiny from modern scholars. However conjectural, a diagrammatic sense of the play's likely "blocking" is immensely instructive and often invaluable. The important thing is a simple awareness of theatrical space and the meaningful employment of this space. This is best achieved by asking ourselves where in the theater a given character, at any moment in the play, must have been; from what position, in what posture, he speaks; and in what relation to others. The suppliant posture, for instance, immediately reveals the relative power of two individuals; when the Chorus in *Oedipus* supplicate the hero, we see not only their dependence but Oedipus's exemption and apparent self-sufficiency. When Euripides' Hecuba and Polymnestor scramble around the orchestra on all fours, animalized by their sufferings, the dramatist is making a crucial modal point about human skills, how they are saved and how destroyed. So too when Sophocles' Philoktetes enters, we see in his taut, bent posture—held erect by the "godlike" bow, pulled down by the "devouring" animal foot—*who* he is and how it is with him, a man in crisis, capable of standing erect as a *man* or falling forever. So too, in *Alcestis*, Admetos' exemption is implicitly contrasted with the hand of death which literally, not merely metaphorically, pulls Alcestis down to Hades; later, when Herakles forces Admetos to take the veiled girl's hand, we are meant to glimpse the gulf that separates him from the earlier, self-sufficient Admetos.

Finally, there remain modal thought and psychology, the *kind* of perception and process by which character in Greek tragedy is perceived, shaped, and altered. The most convenient example is perhaps Aristotle, who (in *Rhetoric* 2, 12-15) gives a penetrating but schematic account of what I would not hesitate to call a modal phenomenology of human age and fortune. The entire section should be read, slowly and medatatively, but even a brief excerpt shows quite clearly the nature of "modal" thought and the distinctions on which it is based:

> Let us now discuss the character of men in terms of their emotions, ages, and fortunes. . . . The ages are youth, the prime of life, and old age. By fortune I mean nobility, wealth, power, and their opposites, and, in general, good fortune and bad.
>
> In character the young are full of desire, and capable of fulfilling their desires. Among bodily pleasures they chiefly obey those belonging to Aphrodite, uncontrollably so. Changeable and quickly surfeited, their desires are excessive but quickly cool; for their wills, like the sick man's hunger and thirst, are keen but not strong. They are passionate, quick to anger, and impulsive. . . . They are eager for honor, but more eager for victory; for youth wants superiority, and victory is a kind of superiority. And they desire both more than they desire money; they have no interest in money because they have not yet experienced need. . . . In character they are high-minded, not suspicious, because they have never seen much wickedness; trusting, because they have seldom been cheated; and hopeful, because the young are naturally as hot-blooded as those who have drunk too much wine. Besides, they have not yet encountered many failures. . . . They have exalted ideas because they have not yet been humbled by life or learned the power of necessity. Moreover, their hopeful disposition makes them think they are equal to great things—and that means having exalted ideas. They would rather do noble deeds than useful ones; their lives are governed more by moral consideration than calculation; it is calculation that aims at the useful, but *aretē* aims at what is noble. . . . All their mistakes lie in the direction of doing things excessively and vehemently. They disobey Chilon's precept by overdoing everything; they love too much and they hate too much and the same with everything else. They think they know everything and confidently assert it; and this, in fact, is why they overdo everything. . . . But if they do wrong, it is because of *hybris*, not wickedness. . . .

Older men . . . have in most cases characters which are just the opposite. . . .

The type of character produced by wealth is visible for all to see. Wealthy men are insolent and arrogant; their possession of wealth makes them think they possess all good things; for wealth is a kind of standard of value for everything else, and so they imagine there is nothing money cannot buy. They are luxurious and ostentatious. . . .

In a word, the kind of character produced by wealth is that of a prosperous fool. At the same time there is a difference between the character of old money and new money; the *nouveaux riches* have all the bad qualities of the type in an exaggerated form; that is, they have not been educated in the use of wealth. The wrongs they do are not caused by wickedness, but partly by *hybris* and partly by self-indulgence. . . .

III

Almost nobody, of course, has ever missed the central modal point of the play—that Admetos learns from Alcestis' death that each man must do his own dying, that death is the ultimate and most personal of facts. Our lives and deaths, moreover, are inseparably linked to those of others: the life Admetos wins by Alcestis' death is, without Alcestis, a life not worth living. No less important, but seldom noticed, is the complementary point on which the play pivots: that human beings *do* in point of fact die for others, that, like Admetos, we permit or compel others to do our dying for us. Self-sacrifice, the voluntary offering of one's life for others or another, has no other meaning, and such sacrifice is a theme which Euripides explores almost obsessively in play after play. The operating premise of the *Alcestis*—implicit in its folktale plot of a man who defers his own death by finding a surrogate—rests upon this simple fact, that individuals and societies constantly ask, and sometimes constrain (as in the case of war or collective expiation), others to do their dying for them. Whether these surrogates are scapegoats like Oedipus, or victims like Pentheus, or volunteers like Alcestis (or Iphigeneia, Makaria, and the others) is less important than the recurrent human situations such sacrifices dramatize. No man, as Admetos learns, can escape his personal death; but we only learn how to live *and* die from those who, by dying *for* others, teach us their value, and ours, and the value of life generally. Men are defined, modally defined, by death; only in the presence of death does life reveal its value. Those who reveal that value best are the heroes—those who, like Alcestis and Herakles, knowingly confront death on behalf of others. The hero, as Nietzsche knew, is the only justification of human life.

That modes are at issue in the themes and assumptions of the plot is self-evident; a play whose immediate subject is a man's schooling in mortality is modal by definition. That everything else in the play—the complex, ramifying structure; the shaping of the characters; the imagery, rhetoric, and logic—are also modal may be less immediately obvious. Certainly the dramatic assumption of the play, on which everything else turns, involves a modal suspension of the law of Necessity (anankē), and the ironic consequence of this suspension is to demonstrate precisely that Necessity cannot be suspended.

For a brief time, Euripides would have us believe, the Fates, thanks to Apollo's stratagem, have become drunk, which is to say that Necessity is still in force but temporarily inoperative. Yet the thematic purpose of this suspension is, ironically, to school Admetos in mortality, the supreme necessity. But no sooner has Admetos accepted death than Necessity is once again ironically suspended in order to permit the "resurrection" of Alcestis. Through the alternating rhythm of these enforcements and suspensions of Necessity, Euripides' play moves in such a way that fabulous, almost fairy-tale, events suddenly take on tragic reality, and tragedy in turn is abruptly metamorphosed into comic fable and parable. It is this rhythm which any reader of the play immediately feels in the pointed contrasting of opposed moods, that chiaroscuro of life and death, comedy and tragedy, that characterize the play. Thus elegiac or funereal scenes are suddenly, often savagely, enjambed with farcical or angry scenes, and this patterning and rhythm are immediately established in the agon of Apollo and Death: the bright savior god confronting the dark lord of the dead. This confrontation is then repeated in the scene in which Pheres and Admetos quarrel before the bier of the dead Alcestis, or in the scene of Herakles' drunken braying in the house of mourning:

There he was, roaring away over his supper . . .
and there we were, mourning for our mistress,
and what with the maids wailing and beating their breasts—
well, you've never heard such a bloody medley in all
your days. . . .

Because in the first scene Apollo tells us that Alcestis will be rescued from death, we are freed from suspense. Deliberately freed, I would argue, so that we can attend to the dramatist's "blocking" of his themes and characters, the metaphysical rhythm of his reversals, and the virtuosity of the play's formal development.

If the structure is clearly modal, so, I think, are the characters. Indeed, they are dramatically shaped in such a way that, once the shaping is perceived, their functional coherence becomes immediately apparent.

What Euripides gives us, I suggest, is a circle of modally defined characters whose initial focus is Admetos. Apollo, Death, Alcestis, Herakles, Pheres, and even the Chorus are dramatically defined in such a way that they all illuminate Admetos and show him for what he is: a man without knowledge of the human modes, without the slightest ability to "think mortal thoughts"; a man of complete modal ignorance and innocence. How, after all, could it possibly be otherwise? Admetos is a *king*; a king whose *wealth* and *good fortune* are painted (at ll 679 ff.)* in almost Croesus-like terms; whose life has been marked by total *exemption* from all circumscribing necessity ("Your luck had been good," say the Chorus to Admetos. "High happiness and great wealth—both were yours. So when this sorrow struck so suddenly, it found you unprepared. Suffering was something you had never known before".) He is a man who possesses a god for a slave, a demigod for friend, and a wife who is willing to die for him. How could such a man, so metaphysically "spoiled," possibly think "mortal thoughts"? How could such a man accept death? Whatever the figure of Admetos may have meant or suggested in pre-Euripidean tradition, in this play he is represented, as so often in Greek literature and life, according to the meaning of his own name.[5] He is Admetos (that is, *a-dametos*, the "untamed," the "unmastered," the "unbeaten": the man unyoked, unbroken by Necessity). It is not an idle coincidence that the Chorus, at line 180, speak of the "dead" as "death-tamed" and "-broken" men (*dmathentas*), and, in the ode on Necessity, declare that *anankē* breaks or subdues (*damadzei*) even the iron of the Chalybes. Admetos, the unbroken man, the unsubdued, will be broken and subdued, forcibly subjected to *anankē*.

That we are intended to see Admetos' character and everything he does as deriving from modal ignorance is made clear, I think, in the remarkable foiling of the *dramatis personae*. We see *who* Admetos is through sharply schematized contrasts in the situations of all the others, including the gods. Thus Apollo, with his opening words, strikes

* Line numbers refer to my English translation unless otherwise indicated.
5. Thus in Sophocles' *Ajax* we find Ajax punning on the meaning of his own name; so too Euripides' Medea and many others. The pun *need* not be explicit. Thus the meaning of Oedipus' name is *visually* evident in the hero's clubfoot; in the Messenger's speech of Euripides' *Hippolytos*, we hear how the hero was literally *destroyed* by his own *horses* and, in his dying, revealed the *other* (fatal) meaning of his name: (*Hippolytos* = "horse-destroyed"). In the *Alcestis* there is, admittedly, no explicit pun on Admetos' name, but the etymological sense could have been brought out at any moment simply by having the actor pronounce the name as "Adametos." At line 416 of the Greek text the poet—deliberately, I think, in order to reveal the meaning of Admetos' name—enjambs it with the word *anankē*.

a starkly modal note. He is that rare, indeed almost unique, thing, a god who has felt the hard stroke of Necessity:

House of Admetos, farewell.
Apollo takes his leave of you,
dear house . . . though it was here that I endured
what no god should be compelled to bear.
Here, with serfs and laborers, I ate the bread
of slavery . . .
                . . . And so,
in punishment, Zeus doomed me,
a god, to this duress,
constraining me to be the bond-slave
of a death-bound man.[6]

The customary order is here reversed, the god occupying the place of the serf, and the mortal Admetos playing the god's master. This modal contrast is then repeated and amplified in the subsequent debate between Apollo and Death. Gods they may be, yet each has his fixed sphere; each is subject to limits he cannot cross. Death possesses the privilege of his office, and he insists that he shall not be denied his due or his prize. Thus his words to Apollo are exemplary modal wisdom: "You cannot have your way in everything you want." True, Apollo finishes by having his way and cheating Death of his prize, but the dramatist's insistence that we should see that even gods have their limits throws Admetos' exemption into sharp relief. But such comparisons—god contrasted with god or mortal, mortal with mortal—are revealingly pervasive, inflecting what the characters say and do, indeed controlling their conception. They exist not as developed or rounded characters in the modern sense, but as masked embodiments of the play's dominant idea as that idea is worked out in the paired tales of Admetos and Alcestis.

Alcestis is initially defined according to the low value assigned to women in fifth-century Athenian society and also, presumably, in the traditional tale of Admetos. In the finale, of course, this low valuation is explicitly challenged and reversed. Her conventional value is low indeed, far below that of her husband; and it is with this conventional valuation that Euripides lulls his audience, deliberately working on its (complacent) expectations, and then startling it into perceiving the story, *his* story and Alcestis', with fresh eyes. In this respect, the modern reader should remember that Admetos' "egotism" and "selfishness" are simply a function of values he shares with the male audience—an audience

6. See Note on lines 1-16.

which would have regarded Alcestis' sacrifice as both plausible and natural. But modally, Alcestis is characterized in terms of the necessity that is hers by virtue of her role as "wife." She is, in the poetic vocabulary of Greek tragedy, a *damar* (i.e. "wife," a word literally meaning "subdued" or "tamed"—derived, revealingly, from the same root as the name "Admetos"). Admetos, we understand, is her "lord and master"; as *damar*, she stands in the same relation to Admetos as does the serf-god Apollo. Around her therefore, especially in her relation to the constraining power of Death, cluster all the modal words of her condition and fate, which she feels as constraint, a weight, a force, a hand pulling her inexorably down.

Herakles also, for the sake of revealing contrast with Admetos, is presented in terms of his subjection to *anankē*. Like Apollo, he too is portrayed as the suffering servant, constrained by his own heroic "labors" and his "lord and master" Eurystheus. In large measure, this Euripidean Herakles is a conventional classical representation; but, conventional or not, the contrast with Admetos is revealing. The hero of exceptional strength the son of Zeus himself—surely Herakles, we think, might reasonably enjoy some degree of exemption from his fate. But no, he too is persistently cast as the very type of patient, toiling, resigned courage. When he first appears, the Chorus' query strikes a modal note (literally, they ask him, "To what wandering are you *yoked?*" Cf. note on l. 571). The yoke which Herakles wears in his lifetime of labors links him closely to the serf-god Apollo and to Alcestis, yoked by marriage to Death. All in fact are yoked to *anankē*, and their collective bondage starkly sets off Admetos' modal exemption. In detail after detail Euripides drives his point home. Thus when the Chorus tells Herakles that the horses of Diomedes will not easily be broken, Herakles answers with something like "stoical" acceptance: "Fighting's what I do./ My labors are my life. I can't refuse." Asked further questions about his labors, he replies: "There you have the story/ of my labors and my life. It's a damned hard road/ I'm doomed to travel, friend. Rough, uphill/ all the way." The contrast with Admetos, especially with the Admetos whose godlike hospitality and good fortune are hailed by the Chorus in the subsequent ode, could hardly be more schematic.

As for Pheres, it is he who, in the coarse, brutal vigor of his speech and his resentment of his overbearing son's behavior, first forces into the open the perception toward which the action has been driving. It is *here*, in this crucial scene (the father-son relationship was peculiarly important in ancient Greek life), that all the previous contrasts, the slow, persistent accumulation of modal detail, surface and erupt. Euripides' strategy here, as I suggested earlier, is to lull his audience with its own (mythical) expectations and then, savagely, to shatter the illusion. It is in this explosive scene between father and son that the traditionally "noble" Admetos is exposed for what he is: a man so modally inexperienced that he cannot assign anyone his just, human value. *Timē* (honor) and *axia* (worth, desert) are recurrent words in this play, and for obvious reasons. Because he is modally ignorant, Admetos is incapable of giving others their due, of valuing them according to their real worth. His values, one might say, are "out of phase"; he treats everybody in the play with quite indiscriminate confusion, making slaves of his wife, his father and mother,[7] and treating Herakles with godlike hospitality but quite without the human candor of a friend (as Herakles later reminds him). Until the arrival of Pheres, however, Admetos' modal ignorance is only implicitly stated in the contrasts between himself and the others.

It is Pheres who brings the poet's purpose in these preceding contrasts into the open, into harsh, angry, public words:

Boy,
who in god's name do you think you are?
Are you my master now, and I some poor, bought,
cringing Asiatic slave that you dare dress me down
like this? I am a free man, Thessalian born,
a prince of Thessaly. . . .
I raised you. I gave you life.
.I am not obliged to die for you as well.

These are strong words in a violently strong speech. They are clearly meant to be strong. Indeed, the scene as a whole aims at outrage. Not because Euripides, as many of his critics would have it, is a sensationalist, interested in showing us a quarrel between two egotists for its own sake, but because the confrontation is crucial to his dramatic conception. In Pheres' words are concentrated all the passion and much of the dignity of ordinary, outraged commonsense. It is Pheres who first openly tells Admetos, with a Greek father's authority, who Admetos is: a modal maniac or simpleton who cannot distinguish between free men and slave, god and man; who does not know what human worth might be because he does not think "mortal thoughts" and who therefore has no human scale of value. We are not required to admire Pheres (indeed, he proves to be ignoble, but not until he has effectively stripped

7. Cf. Euripides, *Frag.* 29 (Nauck), where a character says: "May I never be a friend or associate of that man who, convinced of his own self-sufficiency, regards those dear to him (*philous*) [that is, his family and friends] as his slaves."

Admetos of all claim to aretē); and we cannot dismiss his words simply because they are angry or indecorous. They state, after all, the modal point of the play.

As Admetos stands to Pheres, so he stands to Alcestis and Herakles, ignorant of their true worth, incapable of assigning them the value they clearly assign to him. For it is not only from Apollo's testimony—that Admetos treated him well, as a god deserved to be treated—that we learn of Admetos' intrinsic worth. Alcestis' love, Herakles' friendship, and the Chorus's ambivalent admiration (see 718 ff.) all testify to it. Admetos is not a man of criminal, but innocent, *hybris*. He has a basic liberality of spirit, a child's natural generosity combined with a child's equally natural selfishness. Youth, good fortune, and exemption from all human necessity and need have left him humanly undeveloped, metaphysically "untamed." All his traits of character, quite without exception, derive from his modal innocence and inexperience. "The fortunate man," reads a Euripidean fragment, "must needs be wise." It is precisely wisdom—wisdom as *mortal* skill—that Admetos does not have; and the lack makes him kindred to Euripides' Hippolytos or even Pentheus, whose "godlike" arrogance of youth—their modal ignorance—is their mortal ruin.

Admetos' famous "hospitality" should be understood, I think, as a direct function of his modal ignorance, not as the "redeeming trait" by virtue of which Alcestis is returned to him. The point is fundamental. Both Admetos and the play as a whole will inevitably be "psychologized" by their critics unless we recognize that these characters are not a collection of unconnected "traits" whose only artistic necessity derives from their usefulness to the plot. Ancient dramatic character is not shaped in this random, helter-skelter modern way; rather, everything derives from a central (modal) definition which radiates outward into individual conduct and speech; yet the individual traits inevitably reveal the shaping center from which they spring. A Greek character is in some very real sense a destiny. Admetos' hospitality, like his acceptance of Alcestis' sacrifice, and his rage against Pheres, is a function of his modal exemption; we should see it not as a peculiar, individuating fact but as a direct revelation of a deeper "modal" cause deriving from exemption. Those exempt from suffering and death are, in their "happiness," unmistakably "godlike." And Admetos' hospitality is a divine largesse, a largesse that cannot discriminate and that jumbles all the modes; a generosity matched only and exactly by the ignorance of value which could accept with something like the assurance of a "spoiled" child the offering of another's life. The typical man of *hybris* shows a wanton disregard for others and their human rights. But Admetos' disregard is neither callous nor wanton; he takes because he does not know the cost. And it is precisely the value and the cost that the play will teach him. Even in his hospitality he must learn a human scale, and so, at the end of the play, we find Herakles gently and ambiguously advising him:

. . . in the future treat your guests and those you love
as they deserve.[8]

Admetos is taught "mortal thoughts" by being made to suffer not one necessity, but two. In the *kommos* at lines 1174 ff. he comes to recognize with overwhelming conviction, I believe—that, in losing Alcestis, he has lost his own life. This is what he actually says on several occasions, and in the *kommos* his language is intense poetry, not dialogue. He speaks like a man of sorrows, and we cannot, simply in order to accommodate our modern notions of consistent character, deny his words the dignity of contrition. He is also humiliated, forced on two separate occasions to violate his promise to the dying Alcestis. The first violation occurs in Herakles' "drunken scene," since Admetos had promised Alcestis that he would ban all festivity for the period of a year. The second occurs when Herakles forces Admetos to accept the veiled girl, even though his acceptance means taking a "new woman" into the house. If we are meant to observe the delicacy and punctilio of his scruples, his reluctance and *emotional* loyalty to Alcestis, we are also meant to note his weakness and his eventual surrender to his overbearing friend's insistence. If he does not quite break the *letter* of his promise to Alcestis, it is only because Herakles prevents him from doing so.[9]

The poet's purpose here is the subtle and difficult one of portraying a man torn by conflicting claims—the claims of his dead wife, the claims of his friend; the claims of honor and the claims of need. Unless we can perceive *both* the honor and the need displayed by Admetos *and* his desperate effort to cope honorably with these conflicting claims, the point of the play and the beauty of its finale cannot be understood. Above all, we must be prepared to accept the reality of Admetos' need. For it is his *need* that tells us of his new involvement in necessity and vividly shows him at last thinking "human thoughts." In his effort to

8. See Note on lines 1472-3.
9. The point would not be worth laboring if it were not in question. For a different —in my opinion, quite perversely "archaizing" and, to that degree, insensitive—reading of this scene and the play, cf. A. P. Burnett, *Catastrophe Survived: Euripides' Plays of Mixed Reversal.*

keep his word to Alcestis, to refuse the veiled girl, his honor and his weakness, his nobility and his ordinary need, are beautifully, tensely, balanced. Thus, while Herakles stands there, insistent in his stubborn silence, Admetos says:

As for this woman here,
I beg you, my lord, if you can somehow manage it,
please, take her somewhere else.
Give her to some friend who is not in mourning . . .
But please, please,
don't remind me of my loss. Seeing this woman here,
here in Alcestis' house, day in, day out,
would be more, much more, than I could bear.
I am crushed with sorrow as it is, Herakles.
Do not burden me with more.

Besides,
where in this house could a young girl stay?
I mean, she *is* young, I can see it, Herakles,
in her jewelry, in the style of clothes she wears.
How could she live here, surrounded by young men?
How could I protect her? Young men are lusty,
their desires not easily controlled.
                                        —Herakles,
it is *you*, your interests, I am thinking of.
What can I do? Put her in Alcestis' room?
Take her to Alcestis' bed? . . .
Herakles,
for god's sake, take this woman away,
out of my sight! I am weak now, do not make my weakness
worse. . . .

The leaps and ellipses here are revealing, clearly and economically depicting the passionate motions of Admetos' mind, as he stands there confronted by Herakles' silence and the eloquent presence of the girl who strangely resembles Alcestis. His feelings are all the more powerful because they so obviously derive from the conflicting claims he feels. He will, as his own words suggest, inevitably betray Alcestis (and Herakles), and he is transparently struggling with the foreknowledge of his own weakness, trying, as best he can, to remain loyal to those he loves, as his honor struggles with his need.

That this is Euripides' purpose here is confirmed by the famous "drunken speech" of Herakles. In the intoxicated hero's words, we are given a lively version of what might be called a drunkard's "modalities," the ruddy credo of a man whose drunken wisdom echoes the poetic thought of Archilochos and Bacchylides. *Everything* Herakles says is addressed to the thematic point of the play; it accords completely with the modal knowledge that the play teaches Admetos. Drunkard's wisdom it may be, but it is all of a piece with the play. "C'mere, fella," says Herakles to Admetos' scowling servant, "an' I'll let you in on a l'il secret./ Make a better man of you./ I mean, wise up:/ we all gotta die." And the schooling, the recitation of the play's moral themes, promptly follows:

You know what it'sh like to be a man?
I mean,
d'you really unnerstan' the human condishun, fren'?
. . .
Well, lissen, mister:
we all gotta die. An' that's a fact.
There's not a man alive who knows the odds on death.
Here today. Gone tomorrow.
Poof . . .
Well, that's my message. So what d'you say?
Cheer up and have a l'il drink. . . .
Live for the day. Today is ours.
Tomorrow's fate.
Hey,
an' there's somethin' else. Yup. Aphrodite.
Don't forget Aphrodite, fren'.
'Cause thass a good l'il goddess. . . .
I mean, we all gotta die. Right?
Well, that's why we all gotta think human thoughts,
and live while we can. . . ."

In short, the old contrapuntal themes of the play once again contrasted; the firm, polar music of the opposed necessities—death and life, darkness and light, Thanatos and Apollo, the necessity to accept death and the necessity of living. But in this speech the two themes are related, with the force of *felt* connection: it is only in the presence of death that life takes on value; the recognition of mortality leads directly to the celebration of life. In the words of the poet Archilochos, "Do not exult openly in victory, nor lie at home lamenting a defeat; but take pleasure in what is pleasant; do not yield overmuch to grief, and understand the rhythm that holds mankind in its bonds." It is precisely this "rhythm-in-bonds" that Herakles' drunken speech asserts, and which Herakles will, as friend and moral instructor, impose upon Admetos in the person of the veiled girl, as a temptation and a prize. First comes the acceptance of death, then the acceptance of life (or Aphrodite) which is its "rhythmic" consequence. *Carpe diem*. Death is the starkest manifestation of *anankē*, and men are miserably mortal. *There-*

fore live. Aphrodite, no less than Death, is stamped into a man's nature and defines him, as a contrapuntal part of the great music of Necessity. The man who accepts death must also accept what death implies. This is how men live, "rhythmed in their bonds." Accept, accept; learn the modes by which you live.

This is the music of the play's finale, surely one of the most exquisitely constructed and controlled scenes in all Greek drama. Here we see Admetos tempted and "tamed" by Herakles in a scene of radiantly gentle and understanding friendship. Admetos had earlier implored Herakles not to tempt him or add to his burden of grief by making his weakness worse; now he adjures him not to leave the veiled girl and make him dishonor Alcestis' memory. Of his honor and loyalty to Alcestis, there can be no doubt, just as there can be no doubt of what he has come to recognize:

I lost myself when I lost her. Lost myself—
and so much more.

This is quickly followed by his strong assertion of Alcestis' worth (*axia . . . sebein*) and the loyalty such merit imposes on his honor:

Wherever Alcestis is, she deserves my honor.
I owe it to her.

Indebtedness means need; need implies dependence. In Admetos, the self-sufficient man, such need is especially revealing. Certainly these protestations should not be understood as rhetoric or mere exaggeration; they are *felt*, and felt with especial keenness in the context of Herakles' deft queries and sexual insinuations. Slowly, relentlessly, Herakles lures Admetos on, prodding him into more and more extravagant assertions of loyalty and love, but at the same time subtly tempting him with the veiled girl. His purpose is, of course, to involve Admetos in a public breach (or near-breach) of his word to Alcestis, to add weakness to his weakness in a demonstration of his final infidelity. It is all *force majeure*, beautifully complex modal psychology, whose goal is to school Admetos this time in still another *anankē*, his necessity to live. Its second purpose is friendly revenge—the loving but firmly playful and deliberate revenge of a man of *aretē* on his good friend. If Admetos lets Herakles make a fool of himself in a house of mourning, Herakles now humiliates Admetos by forcing him to welcome a new guest and, by so doing, to break the spirit, if not the letter, of his promise to Alcestis. Thus overbearing insistence and force are met with overbearing insistence and force; humiliation answers humiliation, deception answers deception; and godlike generosity repays divine largesse.

It is very Greek, this precision of "poetic justice": meticulous and pointed, measure for measure. Essential to the scene's power, as I suggested earlier, is the reader's understanding that Admetos is both scrupulously loyal and manifestly tempted. Indeed, it is an index of the dramatist's skill in this scene that loyalty and temptation, strength and weakness, are so delicately balanced and fused in Admetos that we literally cannot tell them apart; they have blended into a single, wholly credible, human figure.

This "temptation" (or comic "taming") of Admetos reaches its climax when Herakles finally provokes Admetos to the point where he declares, in outraged loyalty and virtue:

She is dead.
But I would rather die than betray her love!

Once this is said, Herakles can, with quite disingenuous candor, say: "Nobly spoken, my good Admetos. Well, then,/ make this woman welcome in your generous house." He means, of course, that Admetos has been tested and proven a loyal friend (pistos philos), and noble too; that Herakles can safely entrust the veiled girl to a man of such nobility. And then, in some unmistakable way, having proven his loyalty to Alcestis—by reluctance, by yielding only to a kind of "moral" force— Admetos can rightly, warmly, and humanly weaken, surrendering to his overbearing friend and the necessity represented, as he obviously knows, in the veiled girl standing before him. At last, we see, Admetos thinks "human thoughts"—indeed, all too human thoughts—and this scene of his achieved humanity, his demonstration that he shares the real, right weakness of men and also a stubborn loyalty, is an exceptionally moving thing. Admetos' weakness, true, is ironically intensified, but his discovery of weakness is visibly the source of his human strength for the future. He accepts, as he once did not, the obligations of death and life. He is master of the modes he did not know before; he moves with the rhythm that "holds mankind in its bonds." It is presumably in recognition of this acquired humanity that Herakles relents and reveals the dead Alcestis before Admetos can break his promise by making "a new woman" welcome in his house. There are those who say that Admetos will hear strong words from Alcestis when she is at last permitted to speak. If I am right, and Alcestis understands what she has seen and the change in Admetos, she will not say a word—or nothing more than Shakespeare's knowing Mariana said:

They say, best men are moulded out of faults,
And, for the most, become much more the better
For being a little bad: so may my husband.

IV

Both Alcestis herself and Alcestis' silence are crucial to Euripides' design. Mariana, in Shakespeare's *Measure for Measure*, must *speak* of her husband as she does since, until the fifth act, Shakespeare stresses Angelo's capacity for evil—the *fallen*, rather than the redeemable, Angelo. Then, in his "comic" resolution, Shakespeare deftly "corrects" his earlier emphasis by making Mariana's remarks suggest the richer possibilities of Angelo's one-sided humanity: "They say best men are moulded out of faults": *corruptio optimi pessima*. Euripides, in sharp contrast, completes his schematic but modally rounded account of Admetos (his faults deriving from the same source as his virtues; then his contrition and redemption in decent remorse) *before* the appearance of Alcestis in the finale. It is the fact of Admetos' remorse and self-recognition earlier that makes Alcestis' silence dramatically right and necessary.[10] Miraculously "resurrected," she crowns Admetos' despair with "comic" happiness; by returning from death she "blesses" him. Nothing else—and certainly no speech—is needed. She has died to give him life—and death. What could she possibly say that *her* death and *his* remorse have not already said?

But Alcestis is also there on her own account. She is there to be *seen*, seen for the revelation she is, and which she brings with her, along with her power as a "blessèd spirit" (l. 1355, *makaira daimōn*) to bless others as she has already blessed Admetos, through the challenge and example of her *aretē*. In the nobility of her death, Alcestis wins what, to the Greek mind, all exceptional human action really aims at: the immortality of memory, of memory become myth. Great human action is exemplary and therefore potentially contagious in a culture which everywhere stresses emulation. In Alcestis' "resurrection" here, if the reader is truly attending, everything culminates. That is, at this point the story of Admetos and his "schooling" is suddenly transcended, as

10. Unfortunately, neither Euripides' reticence nor Alcestis' silence have deterred critics from wordy speculations about what Alcestis will say when she is at last allowed to speak. "Surely Euripides meant us to be puzzled by Alcestis' strange silence," writes one scholar (obviously lost in a labyrinth of his own design), "and to ask ourselves the insistent questions his ending poses. What, we want to know, will Alcestis say to Admetos after this latest betrayal? Has Admetos really learned anything at all" etc." The very ability to ask such questions (suggesting a taste nourished on Galsworthy or Christopher Morley) indicates the degree to which naturalism and psychologizing have imposed themselves on Greek drama. Whether the *Alcestis* is "modal" or not, it deserves better than the trudging realism and cozy clichés of modern "domestic" drama which these questions suggest.

the play turns, not so much to Alcestis herself, as to the idea of aretē which, through her, animates the entire action, and which here reaches its final, visual revelation. Dramatically, the movement is crucial. What we get is not merely the happy, comic resolution, but the direct, personal *epiphany* of Alcestis as *hero* and *daimōn*—an epiphany clearly designed, in its *actuality*, in the poet's insistence that Alcestis is, against all doubts, miraculously alive, to reveal the divinity of human aretē. I stress the word "epiphany" (used of course in its proper religious, rather than its borrowed literary) sense.[11] This coda is, unmistakably, a revelation. And revelations, we need to remember, are literally "unveilings": we *see* them, and the evidence of our eyes surpasses any words. So the revelation of Alcestis as hero appropriately crowns a play which tells, against men and exclusive male claims to aretē, of *human* courage revealed in a woman's action.

We moderns must, I suppose, take all this "metaphorically." But Greeks of the classical and archaic period, with their veneration for exceptional human achievement, would, I think, have experienced this coda differently. They would have recognized in it, not metaphor but myth (which is to say, something more serious and true than ordinary or even symbolic reality). Death of course remains irreducibly death, and Alcestis, like her heroic predecessors, clearly goes, in person and in fact, "darkened into death." But against that real physical extinction, the power of myth and memory are strong. So strong in fact that, though physically dead, Alcestis is also, in a very real sense, alive forever: "a blessed spirit," "a shining on the lips of men." In memory and gratitude, the great dead quicken and take on the undying honors of heroes; they become myth and so acquire eternal life. Against the nearly invincible modern notion that myth is a literary conceit or fiction, the reader must make an effort to see these things freshly, with Greek eyes; to understand *how* events happen in mythical time, uniquely and forever, and that "hero" is the name for real *presence*, venerable and abiding, that survives the death of the body. If we cannot recover that Greek feeling for heroism, we must at least be pre-

---

11. Comparison with Shakespeare is, again, revealing. At the close of *The Winter's Tale* Shakespeare "revives" the statue of the "dead" Hermione, makes her descend from her pedestal, and *speak*. The point is not, *pace* Kitto (*Greek Tragedy*, p. 320), that Euripides is "cleverer" than Shakespeare in keeping his heroine silent. Euripides is dramatizing the literal *epiphany*, as *daimōn*, of his heroine, whereas Shakespeare emphasizes the human warmth and reconciliation of a real "recognition-scene" in order that an art that emulates nature may finally be transformed into miraculous nature.

pared to acknowledge its actuality for an ancient audience. Even at the very end of the fifth century, veneration for heroism was strong enough that Sophocles could address his *Oedipus at Kolonos* directly to that understanding. The hero dies; his spirit, his *aretē*, survive him, rich with meaning and sanction for the lives of men; blessing the land that had the wisdom to acknowledge him and make him welcome.

Alcestis' "resurrection" should, I am convinced, be understood in the same way. Euripides, as certain scholars have argued, may have been too skeptical to believe in "the nonsense of physical regeneration." But the point surely is not bodily regeneration but the deathless presence of the hero, the permanance of heroic achivement. That Euripides *did* believe in the immortality of *aretē* seems to me quite beyond dispute; it is explicitly stated and also implied in the structure of plays like the *Herakles* and *Hippolytos* and in the poetic intensity with which he treats it here (above all in the choral "farewell" to Alcestis and, later, in the great ode on Necessity). And Euripides' intent here is, for me at least, strongly confirmed in a parallel passage in his older contemporary Simonides.[12] The pertinent passage is a brief verse epitaph for the fallen heroes of the Persian Wars:

These men crowned their country with glory
and were gathered into the darkness of death.
They died, but are not dead: their courage [aretē]
brings them back in glory from the world below.

Sentiments like these have been too much abused in our own time for us to regard them as anything more than patriotic hyperbole. And the poet may of course be taking advantage of popular belief for his own literary purposes. Against this we should bear in mind the veneration, bordering on religious awe, that Greeks generally felt for the fallen heroes of Salamis and Plataea, and the telling simplicity and sobriety of the poetic epitaph. In any case, what finally matters is the strength of the religious feelings to which the poem appeals, and on which its poetic validity depends. This in fact was how classical Greeks understood heroism—in the firm belief, however paradoxical it may seem to us, that the hero in some real sense survived his own death and

12. The ascription to Simonides may be erroneous, but there is no good reason to question the date or authenticity of the "epitaph." The point is, for my purposes, sufficiently important that I append the last two lines of the text, so that skeptics may test their doubts against the Greek: οὐδὲ τεθνᾶσι, θανόντες, ἐπεί σφ' ἀρετὴ καθύπερθε/κυδαίνουσ' ἀνάγει δώματος 'εξ'Αἴδεω·

achieved the permanence of myth as an exemplary and abiding presence.[13] For my purposes here, that is enough.

Alcestis' resurrection as hero is clearly designed to be dramatically surprising, a stunning comic reversal (*peripeteia*) and *coup de théâtre* (all the more surprising if we take proper account of the male complacency reflected in the traditional handling of the story and presumably represented in the male audience. That reversal has been subtly and elaborately prepared. There are, first of all, the pervasive parallels between Alcestis and the great male culture-heroes who, like her, all confront death or in some sense give their lives for others; Orpheus, Asklepios, and Herakles. So too the obvious dramatic purpose of the "scene" between Admetos and Pheres is that they should disqualify each other as claimants to *aretē* and, by default, leave the dead Alcestis —*meg' ariste*—as the true "heroic" victor of the *agon*—a point tellingly made in the little valediction to Alcestis which closes the scene. Finally there is the ode to Necessity, strategically set just before Herakles' return with the veiled Alcestis.

Here, in this ode, the controlling themes and parallels all powerfully converge as the poet brings his "tragic" action to a close and shows us, unmistakably, how the "comic" finale is to be understood. At the same time, reinforcing the modal themes (and so preparing for the coming reversal, making it, by dint of contrast, more surprising), he declares, with full choral diapason, the iron law of Necessity and death—a bleak, irresistible force deaf to all human prayer and appeal. The chorus of old men—men who, unlike Admetos, have again and again felt the "relentless onset" of *Anankē*—tell that, try as they may, they can discover no remedy against Necessity. All human culture and wisdom are helpless against her; even the Orphic religions which saved men by taking them

13. Perikles, for instance, is reported to have said that the Athenian dead in the Samian War were "immortal as gods" (Plut. *Per*.8, 5). See also the revealing remarks of Plato (*Symposium* 179 b-d) on Alcestis: "Only those who love are willing to die on behalf of others—not only men but women too—a fact which is amply demonstrated for us Greeks by Alcestis, the daughter of Pelias. For only she was willing to die for her husband, despite the fact that he had a father and mother; yet her love so surpassed theirs that they seemed by comparison to be unrelated to their own son and bound to him in name only. But her action seemed so splendid not only to men but to gods that, in recognition of her greatness of spirit, the gods granted what has been given to only the fewest among those who have acted heroically—that her soul should return from Hades. Thus even the gods especially honor *aretē* and devotion in the service of love . . . ." Finally, we should perhaps note the persistence of the Euripidean theme that, if the world were genuinely just and the gods truly cared for human *aretē*, goodness and heroism would be rewarded by rejuvenation and resurrection (cf. the "resurrection" of Iolaos in *The Children of Herakles* and the choral remarks of *Herakles*, ll. 655 ff.).

out of "the wheel of existence," even the remedies of the sons of Asklepios. They endow Necessity with the power of divinity, but a divinity of absolute, pitiless inflexibility:

Mistress, Lady without mercy, I have felt
your stroke before. May you never come again!

As it spoke these words, the Chorus, we must reasonably assume, made the veneration or genuflection which the dread power it invokes as "mistress" or "majesty" (potnia) requires. Necessity may not heed men's prayers, but before that invincible power men must kneel.

Then, in the second strophe, the Chorus turn to Admetos, whom this dreaded "goddess" holds unbreakably in the "bondage of her hands." "Bear it. Be brave" (tolma) advise the Chorus. Bear it because nothing avails. The dead do not return:

Great heroes
die. Even the sons of heaven fade, darkened
into death. . . .

And so it is with Alcestis. "In Alcestis," say the Chorus, "you yoked yourself in marriage to the noblest of women"—meaning: "Then will you be less brave?" And with this the Chorus turn to Alcestis herself:

Do not let Alcestis' grave be numbered
among the ordinary dead. Make her grave a shrine;
honor it as men would honor gods—a holy place
beside the road where those who journey kneel and pray.
The traveler will see her grave and, turning off,
will say of her, "She gave her life to save another.
She is a blessed spirit [makaira daimōn] now, and so may
    also bless."
In homage men will kneel before her grave and pray:
"Hail, Lady, mistress of mercy, by your bravery and love,
bless us and be gracious."

And now, once again, we must imagine, the Chorus go down on their knees in homage, in one of the loveliest examples of visual correspondance in Greek drama. They kneel, seeing in Alcestis the only power that countervails against Death and Necessity—human aretē, human courage and love. And in so doing they explicitly, in their actions, add Alcestis' name to the great roster of those who, like Herakles, have confronted Death and bested it. To the audience, but above all to Admetos, Alcestis is revealed, against all male expectation, as a hero and peer of the great culture-heroes of the past.

V

The *Alcestis* was first performed in 438 B.C. as the final play of a tetralogy consisting of *The Cretan Women, Alkmaion in Psophis,* and *Telephos* (none of which has survived). Euripides won second place. If the *Cyclops* and *Rhesos* are not, as some scholars suppose, early plays, then the *Alcestis,* written when the dramatist was in his forties, is the earliest play by Euripides we possess. It is also unique of its kind. Since it does not possess the requisite chorus of satyrs (as does the *Cyclops*), it cannot be called genuine "satyr-drama." Yet it *did* occupy the *place* of the satyr-play which, in the dramatic festivals of Dionysos, traditionally rounded off a tragic trilogy (or trio of otherwise unconnected tragedies). And it also clearly displays some of those sportive and farcical characteristics (above all in Herakles' drunken speech and the happy resolution) which led one ancient critic to describe "satyr-drama" as "tragedy-at-play." Hence it is customary now to call the *Alcestis* a "pro-satyric" play, although this tells us very little since we possess no other example of that genre (except perhaps the *Orestes*). In the circumstances it seems best to accept Professor Dale's judgment that the *Alcestis* possesses a greater range and variety of mood than any extant work by any of the three ancient tragedians, and that it would be foolish to press the definition of genre beyond that point. It may be that Euripides invented the genre or adapted a traditional form in a new way; but we simply do not know. What we do know is that the *Alcestis* is the first Western drama that can truly be called "tragicomic"; the first work in a genre that runs from this play to the Euripidean *Ion, Iphigeneia at Tauris,* and *Helen,* to Shakespeare's *Measure for Measure* and the late "comedies," to Chekhov and, finally, in our own time, to such Euripidean "imitations" as T. S. Eliot's *The Cocktail Party* and *The Confidential Clerk.*

VI

Like every recent translator of the *Alcestis,* I am deeply indebted to the work of the late A. M. Dale whose splendid Oxford text (and commentary) is, in my opinion, one of the very few editions of Euripides in which fine scholarship is guided and controlled by high literary intelligence. Certainly her edition is a milestone in the scholarship of this play, and, even in those instances when I have disagreed with her readings or interpretation, I have constantly found illumination and help in her work.

To my wife who made many valuable suggestions and who gently suffered through my theatrical *viva voce* renderings of successive drafts of each episode and chorus, I owe the *charis* which her patient support and many suggestions merit. To my colleague D. S. Carne-Ross I am grateful for criticism and advice. To my students at Boston University and Brooklyn College and elsewhere, who provided me with the intelligent responses of a captive audience, I am deeply grateful. Finally, to Ann Dargis who, with unfailing good cheer and diligence beyond the call of duty, typed, and constantly retyped, the manuscript, I owe a great debt of thanks.

Lincoln, Vermont

WILLIAM ARROWSMITH

1974

ALCESTIS

CHARACTERS

APOLLO
DEATH
CHORUS of Old Men of Pherai
LEADER of Chorus
MAID to Alcestis
ALCESTIS wife of Admetos
ADMETOS king of Pherai
HERAKLES
PHERES father of Admetos
SERVANT

Line numbers in the right-hand margin of the text refer to the English translation only, and the notes at p. 97 are keyed to these lines. The bracketed line numbers in the running head lines refer to the Greek text.

The scene is Pherai, chief city of Thessaly. The stage building represents the palace of ADMETOS, *king of Thessaly. In the center is a large double-doored entrance, flanked by two lateral doors; one door leads to the women's quarters, the other to the men's.*

Enter APOLLO, *with traditional bow and quiver, from one of the lateral doors. He walks toward the steps leading to the orchestra, then stops and makes his farewell to the house.*

APOLLO House of Admetos, farewell.
     Apollo takes his leave of you,
     dear house . . . though it was here that I endured
     what no god should ever be compelled to bear.
     Here, with serfs and laborers, I ate the bread of slavery.

                        He turns to the audience.

     I do not blame Admetos.
     The author of my shame was Zeus. He killed
     my son Asklepios, stabbing him through the heart
     with his fatal lightning. And I in anger
     retaliated. I killed the one-eyed Cyclopes   10
     because they forged for Zeus those blazing bolts
     in which my son died. And so,
     in punishment, Zeus doomed me,
     a god, to this duress,
     constraining me to be the bond-slave
     of a death-bound man.
     He drove me here, to this country of Thessaly,
     where I served as cowherd for a good and generous man—
     a man who is now my friend—Admetos.
                        Until today
     I guarded this house from every evil thing,   20
     loyally and well. It was I who saved Admetos

33

from sentence of death. He was doomed to die young,
but I outwitted the Fates and won him a reprieve:
Admetos' day of death might be deferred
if someone else would volunteer to take his place
below. One by one he asked them all,
all those who were bound to him by ties of love,
but no one would.
His father and mother were old, and he was theirs,
but even they refused. Everyone refused.   30
All but one: his wife Alcestis.
Only she
would volunteer to leave the sweet light of the sun
and take his place below.
                              She is dying now.
Her women are holding her, but she is sinking
in the final agony of death. This is the day,
the fatal day, and she must die.
                              And now
I take my leave of this dear house which sheltered me
and which I love. Death must not pollute
my bright divinity.
                        Look: already
the god of Death, the god who consecrates the dead   40
is here to take his victim to the world below.
He has been waiting for this day with great impatience.
And now Death is here, punctual as always,
at the appointed hour.

APOLLO *descends to the orchestra and moves toward the east-*
ward exit. From the west DEATH *appears, a grim and winged fig-*
ure, shrouded in black and carrying a naked sword. Startled to
discover APOLLO, *he stops short, and the two gods face each*
other in tense confrontation on opposite sides of the orchestra.

DEATH You here,
          Bright One,
          meddling with this house again?
          Have you returned

to violate again the dues and honors
of the gods below?   50
You cheated the Fates
by craft and guile.
You saved Admetos from death.
And now, bow in hand,
unsatisfied and unappeased,
you come in violence
to save Alcestis too.
Didn't she give her solemn word
to take Admetos' place?

APOLLO Don't be afraid, Death.   60
       My principles are fair, and I have reason on my side.

DEATH If you have reason on your side, then why the bow,
       Apollo?

APOLLO   The bow is my attribute and habit.
       Where I go, it goes.

DEATH   Your habit, is it?
       Like your habit of always favoring this house?
       Is *that* your principle?

APOLLO   Admetos is my friend.
       The troubles of those I love constrain me too.

DEATH Then you mean to take Alcestis by force?

APOLLO I did not take Admetos. Not by force.

DEATH Then why is he still here, among the living,   70
       when he belongs below?

APOLLO   He gave you his wife.
       You came to get Alcestis, didn't you?

DEATH   I did.
And she is *mine*, Apollo. Where I go, she goes:
beneath the earth.

APOLLO   Take her then.
                                      No, wait, Death . . .

DEATH Wait?
To kill those doomed to die? Don't teach me my office,
Apollo.

APOLLO   Defer her death.

DEATH   Ah, I see. Go on.

APOLLO Let Alcestis grow old. Let her live,
I adjure you, Death.

DEATH   Never.
I have my dues and honors too, Apollo,
as dear to me as yours to you.   80

APOLLO One life is all you get. Young or old,
what difference does it make?

DEATH   Honor.
The younger my victim, the more mankind fears me
and respects me.

APOLLO   Think it over, Death.
Let Alcestis die old, and her funeral will be rich.
The profit is yours.

DEATH   Spoken like a plutocrat, Apollo.
You legislate in favor of the rich.

APOLLO   Amazing.
This talent for quibbling, this shyster wit—
it's not what we expect of Death.

36

DEATH The rich would buy immunity from dying.   90

APOLLO Then you refuse my appeal?

DEATH   I do. Irrevocably.
       You know my stubborn nature.

APOLLO   All too well.
       Men hate you for it. The gods despise you

DEATH Even you must learn a limit, Apollo.
       You cannot have your way in everything you want.
       You will not have it now.

APOLLO Death, Death, all your savagery
       is not enough to help you now.
       Today, now,
       a man is coming to Admetos' house.   100
       A man, I say. Man enough
       to break the wild stallions of Diomedes
       and herd them home from frozen Thrace.
       That man will find a welcome in this house.
       He will fight with you and break you, Death,
       and by brute strength bring Alcestis back.
       You shall honor my appeal against your wish.
       You shall not have my thanks.
       My hatred you shall have. You have it now.

                              Exit APOLLO *to the east.*

DEATH Bluster away, Apollo.   110
       Words will get you nowhere.

       *He moves toward the central door of the palace, then turns
                       and addresses the audience directly.*

       This woman must go beneath the earth.
       She is mine.

With this sword I now inaugurate my rite.
The head whose curls are cut by this bright blade
is consecrated to the gods below:
forever.

DEATH *enters the palace through the central door. The doors*
close slowly behind him. There is a prolonged silence. Then
the CHORUS *of old citizens of Pherai enter the orchestra, throng-*
ing around the entrance to the palace.

LEADER So still. . . . I wonder what this silence means.
Why is the great house so strangely quiet?
No one at the door, no servant here
to say the queen has died and we must mourn her.   120
Or is Alcestis still alive?
Let her live!
If bravery and love deserve the light,
no woman on this earth,
                              oh Alcestis,
ever less deserved to die!

CHORUS (*speaking individually*)
—Silence. . . .
                    —do you hear the cry of women?
—The beating of women's hands?
—Or women keening with that cry
that says—
              —everything is over?
—Nothing.   130
              —Nothing.
—Silence still.
—And no servant stationed at the door. . . .
—O Paian, lord of healing!
—Great Apollo,
                    come,
calm this storm of sorrow.

—But if the queen had died,
the house would shrill with grief,
the high, shrill cry of sorrow.
—Dead, dead. . . .
                    —She must be dead,
but not yet buried.   140
—What makes you so certain?
—How could Admetos bury such a wife
with no friends or mourners by?
—Surely he could not do it.
—Not a woman like this. . . .
—Not Alcestis!

—And where is the cleansing water
custom prescribes for a house of death?
—There is no water at the door. . . .
—And no locks of hair   150
hang in the courtyard
to honor the dead. . . .
—No cry of women keening. . . .
—But this is the day decreed.
—Decreed?
            —The day of death.
—Hateful word!
—It hurts, it hurts.

LEADER As it must.
        When the good are hurt, those who love them suffer too.
        We love, and love hurts.

CHORUS —Take ship and search the world: there is   160
        no harbor, landfall, haven, hope;
        no oracle or pilgrimage a man might go
        and, going, save our lady's life.
        None:
        Not in Lykia where the shining god

39

sings to mortal men his convalescent song.
Not Sahara where, at holy Ammon's
healing touch, the dying desert makes
a miracle of green. But not for her,
whose death shows cruel and sheer
as crag or stone, where hope holds not,   170
and prayer no purchase has,
and god is still,
and all's despair.

—There was one hope: Asklepios, Apollo's
healing son. If *he* still saw the light;
if he were here, he might have brought her
back,
alive from Hades and the long black
home. Such was his skill and craft
he medicined to life and saved
death-tamed and -broken men,   180
redeeming all—until great Zeus,
enraged with man's contriving mind,
hurled the long white flash of fire in which
the healer perished with his art.
And now I see of hope no
sign. None. Nothing
but despair.

—All that kings might do, our king has done.
Everywhere, on all the altars of the gods,
the blood of sacrifice runs black. But
this disease is mortal. It has no cure.   190

LEADER Look:
a servant girl is coming out.
She is crying. . . .
Now we shall know the truth.

Enter MAID *from the palace, weeping. At the sight of the
elders of the* CHORUS, *she tries to stifle her sobs.*

No need to hide your tears, child.
If anything has happened to your mistress,
your sorrow is only natural.
But tell us: is Alcestis still alive?

MAID What can I tell you? She is still alive.
And dead.

LEADER   What are you saying, child?

MAID Sir, the queen is dying. . . .   200

LEADER   Oh, Alcestis, Alcestis!
What a loss. Poor Admetos, how I pity him. . . .

MAID The master does not know the meaning of his loss.
He will not know, until it is too late.

LEADER Nothing can be done to save her?

MAID   Nothing.
This is the day. Her destiny is too strong,
a force she cannot fight.

LEADER   Admetos—

MAID   Did all he could.
Her women are working, preparing for the funeral.
She will be buried as we knew her and loved her
in this life: a queen.

LEADER   In dying and living both:
incomparably a queen. For courage and love   210
Alcestis has no rival among all women
on this earth.

MAID   Rival?
                    What would the woman be who could rival
or surpass Alcestis? What woman ever loved a man so much?
Loved him more than herself? So much more
she gave her life to let him live? In love
she has no equal, sir: the whole world knows it.
But what she did and said, in privacy, inside—
her bravery and beauty in the face of death—
will touch your heart and amaze you even more.
                                                        Listen:
This morning, when she knew her day had come,   220
she bathed her white body in fresh running water
from the river. Then she opened the great cedar chest,
took out her richest, finest things and dressed herself
in all her loveliness—oh, sir, she was beautiful!
And then she kneeled,

(*kneeling*)
                    like this,
                                        before the hearth
and prayed:
                    "Bright goddess who guards my home,
I am going to the world below. This is the last time
I shall ever kneel at your feet. Lady, I pray you,
protect my children and be good to them.
Give my little boy a loving wife.   230
And give my girl a kind and gentle husband.
Do not let them die like me, before their time
has come. Let them live out their lives; let them be happy
here in the land of their fathers."
Then she went from altar to altar, praying at each one
and wreathing it with sprays of fresh myrtle; quietly,
not a sound, not a cry, that sweet face of hers
composed and calm, oh, as though no evil thing
could ever touch her.
                    But there in her room
she threw herself on the great bed, and the sobs   240
broke from her. "Dear bed," she cried,

42

"it was here I offered my maiden body and my love
to Admetos. Now I offer him my life. . . .
Sweet bed, I love you still . . . even now. So much
that I would rather die than live without you
both. And now it is goodbye. . . .
Some other girl will sleep here in my place
perhaps—not more loving, not more loyal, than me,
but happier, much happier, I think.
Then she kneeled,   250
                    —so—
                              and kissed the bed,
smothering it with tears, crying uncontrollably,
till there were no tears left. Then she rose
and stumbled, head down, groping for the door.
On the sill she stopped and turned, hesitating,
then threw herself back on the bed again. There,
on the bed, the children found her. Sobbing,
they clung to their mother's dress, while she pulled them
to her, hugging and kissing: goodbye, goodbye.
Then the servants came crowding around, mourning.
No one there, not even the meanest, was forgotten.   260
Graciously, simply, she gave her hand to each
and said goodbye.
                              This is what
Admetos' house has lost. What has he gained but life?
If he had died, he would have lost Alcestis.
Now, as matters stand, he has lost her anyway.
As long as he lives, his life will have that taste
of pain and loss—a bitterness that lasts.

LEADER It is a great loss—a loss whose anguish
          he must be suffering now.

  MAID   Yes, he is crying,
          holding his wife in his arms, imploring her   270
          not to leave him, not to die, madly
          wanting what cannot be,
          while she lies there, a dead weight

43

in his arms, all white and wasted
with that dying sickness.
She can barely breathe,
but with what little breath she has,
she is calling for the light,
the light she'll never see again.
She wants the light: 280
                    the light! the light!
a last look at the sun's sweet light.
But, sir, I'll go
and announce your presence.
It isn't everyone who cares about this house
or is ready to share our sorrows with us.
But you have always been a good and loyal friend,
and, sir, you're welcome here.

                              Exit MAID *into the palace.*

CHORUS —Is there no answer, Zeus?
         No way? Must it be disaster?

         —Answer our prayers, O Lord!   290
         Or must we put black mourning on?

         —We must, we must. But first, friends,
         pray to the gods. Their power is great.

         (*kneeling*)

         O Paian, power of healing, come!
         Apollo, have pity on this house!
         Lord, give us life
         as once you conquered Death
         and let Admetos live.
         Now Death has come to take his queen.

Apollo, lord,   300
       beat back this ruthless,
savage god of Death!

—I pity you, Admetos. How, without Alcestis,
can you live at all?

—O gods,
in bitterness for this,
a man might cut his throat
or twist the rope around his neck
and hang himself for grief
in heaven's holy face.

—Not for love,
but something more than love,   310
Alcestis dies for you today,
oh Admetos!

LEADER Look, here comes the queen Alcestis,
with king Admetos at her side.

> ALCESTIS, *supported by* ADMETOS *and maids, appears from the*
> *palace, followed by the two children. Attendants bring on a*
> *litter which they place near the door.*

CHORUS O land of Pherai mourn
and let the wounded Earth cry sorrow;
no nobler woman ever lived
and yet she goes   fading   dying
wasted
         down
            to the world below.

LEADER Do not say that marriage has more happiness than pain.
I have seen too many marriages.   And now I see   320

the torment of this house: this bravest of women
dying, and a king in agony. As long as he lives,
his life will taste of death,
all he will have is hell.

ALCESTIS (*stretching out her arms in longing to sun and sky*)
O Sun
Sweet shining light
white clouds swelling   wheeling in the blue

ADMETOS The god of light looks down and sees us suffering.
Why, why? How have we hurt the gods that you should die,
Alcestis?

ALCESTIS (*slumping down, head forward, faintly*)
Sweet earth of Iolkos   O earth   330
where I was born   O house that sheltered me
where I was a girl
in Iolkos

ADMETOS (*lifting her up and supporting her*)
Up, Alcestis. Stand. Live. Don't leave me now.
Pray. The gods are strong. What they will is done.
Implore the gods, for pity's sake, to let you, please,
let you live.

ALCESTIS I see the black water and the dead
lake   the boat beached on the sand
and look
           Charon
                 there at the rudder
calling me   Why are you waiting Alcestis?   340
It is time to leave   hurry Alcestis
come
         Don't you hear him calling?
So angry and impatient

ADMETOS This is a bitter crossing. It is bitter for us both,

Alcestis. O gods, what have we done that we should suffer
so?

ALCESTIS No!   a hand   someone   something
holding me hard, forcing me down

                                            down

to the dead world—

                        So dark   And look
those black eyes glowing   those great black wings
beating over me   350

                    it is Death!   Death!
how terribly he frowns   No no
please   no   let me go   I won't
let me go   the road is dark
I am so afraid

ADMETOS For all who love you, dear, for the children and me,
this is a dreadful journey. We are afraid for you,
afraid for us all.

ALCESTIS Admetos let me down   let me lie
down   I am too weak to stand
Death is closing in   my eyes are going   350
dark

                        A silence. Then she clutches the children to her.
O children
goodbye
you have no mother any more
I love you   the light is yours   children
be happy in the light

ADMETOS Goodbye—
Oh, gods in heaven, I would rather die
than hear you say that dreadful word!
Oh, if you could find the strength to speak that hard and bitter
                word to me,
then find the strength to stay!
Oh Alcestis

for our children's sake   for me
be strong   be hard   stand   370
fight it   live
your dying is my death
in you we live in you we die
by your love we pray you

(*kneeling*)

live

ALCESTIS Admetos, I am dying.
This is my last request of you, so listen well.
Of my own free will I gave my life
to let you live. I am dying for you, Admetos,
but I did not have to die.
I could have chosen otherwise. As your widow   380
I might have married any man in Thessaly
and lived with him here and ruled this royal house.
But without you, with these children fatherless,
I could not live. I am young, Admetos,
but I have given you my youth—the good years,
the happy years. All the others failed you.
Your father and your mother would have let you die,
though they had lived good lives and reached an age
when death comes naturally and right. There was glory too,
for them, in giving up their lives to save their son.   390
For they had no other sons, and no hope of any
after you. They could have died for you,
and you and I would still have lives to live.
You would not be left alone to mourn for me,
and our children would have a mother. . . .
                                        Why?
Who knows? Some god has brought these things to pass.
Let it be.
                Now, Admetos, I want your promise.
It is a little thing I ask you, nothing much—
oh, nothing like the gift of life I gave you,

since that's a gift that has no price. No,   400
a small request, but one I have a mother's right to ask,
and you, I think, a father's heart to grant. Surely
you love these children, Admetos, as much as I.
Oh, if you love them, make them masters in this house;
do not take a second wife and make her mistress here
where she may do our children harm because they're mine,
and she is jealous.
                    Oh promise me, Admetos, promise me.
Swear to me no woman will ever enter
through that door again. A new wife hates the children
of the old, hates them with a viper's poison.   410
The boy will have his father to protect him.
                                    —But you,
poor girl, what will your childhood be like,
if your father marries a second wife? Will she be kind
while you are growing up? Or will she make up stories
out of spite and spoil your hopes of marriage, spoil
your wedding day when I will not be there
to take your side? Not be there to hold your hand and help
in childbirth, when a girl most needs her mother's love
and help. . . .
                    I will not be there. I have to die.
Oh, not tomorrow, not the next day, not this month,   420
but now, in just a minute, I will not be here
with you at all.
                    Goodbye   I love you very much
Be happy
                    Admetos   be proud of me   you can.
Children   remember your mother   remember my example
be brave

LEADER I will vouch for Admetos.
He is a noble man. He will keep his promise.

ADMETOS You have my word, my solemn promise.

(*solemnly raising his right hand*)

I swear it.
Oh Alcestis,
living or dead you are my wife.
I love you, I will always love you. 430
Only you.
No other woman will ever live with me again.
There is no woman in this world of Thessaly
by birth so noble or in looks so lovely,
none, none who could ever take your place
in my home or heart.
Your children are ours; I want no more.
I only pray the gods will let them live
for me to cherish and enjoy:
they are all I have of you.
I will mourn you, not the customary year, 440
but all my life.
Those whose cowardice has caused your death,
my father and mother, will have my hatred, always.
Their love was only words: a lie.
You were loyal in love. You alone, Alcestis.
You loved me so you gave your life, your only life,
to let me live.
I know what I have lost, how much,
and I will mourn you as your love and mine deserve.
Here and now I banish from this house
all festivity. The happiness that filled these rooms— 450
good cheer and gaiety, the table where I sat and drank with
            friends,
the joy of music, flowers—all of them I banish now
forever. I used to play the lute, but I will never
touch its strings again. Let the flute I loved
be still.
Oh, Alcestis, all my joy in life is gone
with you!
How can I hold you here, a little of you, still?
Listen:
I'll have an artisan of cunning skill
contrive your likeness for our bed, and at night

I'll lie beside it, dreaming you are there
and whispering your name. . . .   460
                              Cold comfort, I know,
but I have nothing else. Even seeming helps.
You would come to me at night, often, in dreams,
and I would have, if only for a while,
the satisfaction of the love I used to have
in life.
               In life. . . .
                         Oh, Alcestis,
if I had the song and poetry of Orpheus
so I could charm the god of Hell, bewitch his queen
and, by my singing, spell you back from death,
I'd go beneath the ground. Nothing would stop me,
not Kerberos himself or Charon bending   470
at his fatal oar could stop me from bringing you back
to life.

               Wait for me below. Wait until I die.
Make a house for us, where we can be together.
I'll have our bodies buried in a cedar coffin,
side by side. In death I will never
leave your side, since only you were true in life.
You stood beside me to the bitter end.

LEADER   Admetos,
I will stand beside you now, as friends should stand,
and we will mourn your wife together.
All our grief combined is less than she deserves.   480

ALCESTIS Children, you have heard your father give his word.
He will never make another woman welcome in this house.
He will honor my memory.

ADMETOS I promised.

        (*raising his right hand*)

And I will keep my promise.
I swear it.

ALCESTIS   Then give me your hand.

She takes his right hand and formally delivers the children to
his keeping.

Now take these children and love them

ADMETOS   I do.
I love the gift as I love the giver.

ALCESTIS love them as their mother loved them

ADMETOS   I must.
I will love them as their mother would have loved them,
had she lived.   490

ALCESTIS   Oh   I should have lived   not died.
My poor children

ADMETOS   How can I live without you?

ALCESTIS Time will dull your grief   the dead are nothing

ADMETOS Take me with you, Alcestis! For god's sake,
let me die. . . .

ALCESTIS   My dying is enough   Admetos
I am dying for you.

ADMETOS   Stay with me. . . . Stay. . . .

ALCESTIS Darkness now   so heavy   my eyes are closing

ADMETOS What am I, Alcestis, without you? Nothing.

ALCESTIS I am nothing now   the dead are nothing

ADMETOS Lift your head, Alcestis. Look at your children.
How can you bear to leave them?   500

ALCESTIS (*raising her head with a final effort*)
                                        I have to leave them
        Goodbye   children

ADMETOS   Look at them! *Look!*

ALCESTIS Ahh
                                She sinks down on the litter, dead.

ADMETOS What are you doing? No . . . no . . . no . . .

LEADER She is dead, Admetos.

        (*to the* CHORUS *and audience*)

                        —The queen is dead.

        *Sobbing and crying, the children throw themselves on the body
                of their mother, while* ADMETOS *tries to comfort them.*

ADMETOS She cannot hear you, she cannot see you.
        Poor motherless children. . . .
                                O gods in heaven,
        this is beyond bearing. . . .

        Crumbling in grief, he joins his children beside the bier.

LEADER It had to be, Admetos. All we can do with death
        is bear it patiently. Be brave. You are not the first
        to lose a loving wife; you will not be the last.
        We were born to die.   510

53

ADMETOS   I know. . . . Day after day
I saw it coming on, those great wings like a black shadow
swooping down. And waiting, just waiting—
oh, if you knew the agony of it.

(*with an effort controlling himself*)

                              But no more.
I must give orders for the funeral.

(*to the* CHORUS)

                              —Good friends,
I need your presence and support. Help me
by remaining here. Raise a song in honor of Alcestis,
and by the beauty and the power of your singing,
cry defiance to this hard and bitter god
whom nothing will appease but death.

(*to audience*)

                              —To my subjects
I now proclaim a period of solemn public mourning   520
for your queen. Shear your hair in sign of sorrow,
put on mourning black. Let my cavalry and guard
crop their horses' manes. Throughout this city
let the lyre be still; let no one touch a flute
until twelve moons have waxed and waned and brought the year
full circle.
              I shall never bury anyone I loved
so much, nor anyone who loved me more. Only she
would take my place in death, and she shall have from me
the honor she deserves.

The servants raise the litter holding the body of ALCESTIS *and
carry it inside the palace, followed by* ADMETOS *and the two*
                                                    children.

CHORUS Farewell, Alcestis. Our loves goes with you now   530
        beneath the earth to your long home among the tribes
        of those on whom the sweet light never shines: unseeing
        and unseen. We shall not see your like again.
        O Death, in that dark tangle of your mind, if you have
        eyes to see, look among the herded dead who go
        with Charon in his long slow crossing over Acheron;
        look and you will see, blazing in that crowd of ordinary
        dead, the noblest life the sunlight ever shone upon!

        You shine in memory. And mortal men, remembering
        you, will praise your death: a song that does not die.   540
        Each year, unaccompanied, your song shall rise,
        a shining on the lips of men; or sometimes chanted
        to the rude and simple lyre, at Sparta when the year
        has come full circle, and the moon, a splendor, rides
        the livelong night; or there in Athens' blazing noon.
        Wherever there is light, wherever men remember love,
        Death shall not eclipse the glory of your shining.

        I am old, too old. Oh, if the strength were mine
        to bring you back, I'd go below and break the stubborn
        grip of Hell, where Charon, toiling, bends his body   550
        to the dead stroke of the sad oar slowly beating
        over Acheron. So beautiful in love, so strong
        and brave, you gave your life to take his place in death!
        For love you went below. Rest peacefully, Alcestis.
        Earth, lie gently on her grave, for she was gentle always.

LEADER Lady, if Admetos ever loves again,
        he will have your children's hate and mine. He will have it
        always.

CHORUS They were old, so old, his father and his mother, both
        blanched with age, both in the winter of their years.
        Old, so very old. But still they grudged their bodies   560

to the grave. Old cowards, grasping at the light,
so greedy still to live! Though he was theirs, their own,
those old ones would not die. But you, Alcestis, you,
in the fresh morning of your days, you gave your life
and took Admetos' place below. You died for love.
For such a love as yours, I would give my very life!

LEADER Unselfish love, like hers, is rare. So rare
that I would want her at my side, alive. I would love her
always.

Enter HERAKLES *from the left. Dressed in his familiar lion-skin and armed with his bow, he is immediately recognized*
by the CHORUS.

HERAKLES I give you greetings, elders of Pherai.

(*to* LEADER)

—Old sir,
is king Ametos here?

LEADER   He is, Herakles. But tell me:
what business brings you to Thessaly?

HERAKLES   Obligation, friend.
I have a labor to perform. Eurystheus is my master.
He commands, and I obey.

LEADER   What is your mission?
And where are you bound?

HERAKLES   A long, hard journey.
My destination's Thrace. My orders are to capture
Diomedes' horses.

LEADER   Diomedes' horses? It can't be done,
Herakles. Surely you've heard of Diomedes?

HERAKLES No. Nothing. I've never been in Thrace before.

LEADER Those horses are wild. They can't be broken.

HERAKLES Can't be broken?   580

LEADER   Not without a fight, they can't.

HERAKLES Fighting's what I do.
My labors are my life. I can't refuse.

LEADER But with Diomedes, it's kill or be killed.

HERAKLES I've confronted Death before.

LEADER   Suppose you kill him:
what will it get you?

HERAKLES   Why, I get his horses.
And what I get, Eurystheus gets.

LEADER   It won't be easy
to put a bridle on those jaws and curb those teeth.

HERAKLES What's so hard? Are they fire-breathing monsters,
or just plain horses?

LEADER   Wild horses, Herakles. Killers.
Cannibal horses, with teeth so sharp and fast   590
they can slice a man to ribbons.

HERAKLES   To hear you tell it,
they sound like tigers, not a team of horses.

LEADER You should see their mangers. Caked with human blood.

HERAKLES So Diomedes bred these pretties, did he?
And who does Diomedes claim to be? Who bred him?

LEARED His father was the war-god Ares, or so he boasts.
He commands, as king, the golden cavalry of Thrace.

HERAKLES Ares' son, is he? There you have the story
of my labors and my life. It's a damned hard road
I'm doomed to travel, friend. Rough, uphill   600
all the way. One after another
I've had to fight every bastard son the war-god ever had.
First it was Lykaon. Then Kyknos. And now
this confrontation with the master of this pack
of killer horses. But no man on this earth
has ever seen the son of Alkmene flinch from a fight.
No one ever will.

LEADER   Here comes king Admetos now
to welcome you in person.

Enter ADMETOS *from the palace. His hair is cropped and he is
dressed in mourning black.*

ADMETOS   Welcome, Herakles.
Son of Zeus, welcome to my house.

HERAKLES   Heaven smile
on you and yours, Admetos!   610

ADMETOS   If only it had. . . .
But thank you, Herakles. I know you mean well.

HERAKLES Why is your hair cut? Are you in mourning?

ADMETOS There has been a death in my house, Herakles.
The funeral is today.

HERAKLES   I hope nothing has happened
to your children.

ADMETOS   No, thanks be to heaven,
my children are alive and well.

HERAKLES   Your father then?
If so, he lived a long, full life, Admetos.

ADMETOS My father is well. My mother too.

HERAKLES   Not Alcestis?
Surely not Alcestis?

(*a long pause*)

ADMETOS Yes. . . .   620

(*a short pause, then quickly*)

No.

HERAKLES   What in god's name are you saying,
Admetos? Is she alive or is she dead? Which?

ADMETOS Both. Both. I am in agony, Herakles . . .

HERAKLES   Alive
and dead? But these are riddles, Admetos.
Make sense.

ADMETOS   You know that she was doomed to die?

HERAKLES I know she promised to take your place below.

ADMETOS Knowing what she promised, knowing she is doomed,
how can I think of her as still alive?

HERAKLES   Ah . . .
Wait until she dies, Admetos. Don't mourn her yet.

ADMETOS Those who are doomed are as good as dead.
And the dead are nothing.   630

59

HERAKLES   There is a difference
between life and death. Or so men think, Admetos.

ADMETOS That is your opinion, Herakles. Not mine.

HERAKLES Then why are you in mourning? Clearly
someone has died, someone you loved, Admetos.
Who?

ADMETOS   A woman, Herakles. A woman has died.

HERAKLES Was she related to you?

ADMETOS   Not by blood.
But there were bonds . . . The attachment was strong.
We loved her very much.

HERAKLES   Why was she living here?

ADMETOS After her father's death, she was left an orphan.
We took her in.   640

HERAKLES   I am sorry for you, Admetos.
I have come at a bad time, it seems.

                          He shoulders his bow and turns to leave.

ADMETOS What are you doing, Herakles?

HERAKLES   'Leaving, Admetos.
I have other friends in these parts. I'll stay with them.

ADMETOS Impossible, my lord. I won't have it.
I won't hear of it.

HERAKLES   Your house is in mourning.
A guest would only be a burden.

ADMETOS   The dead are dead.

(taking HERAKLES by the arm and forcibly detaining him)

I insist.
        You must stay.

HERAKLES   It wouldn't be right, Admetos.
    This is a time for mourning, not entertaining friends.
    You cannot do both at once.

ADMETOS   The guest rooms are separate.
    I'll put you there.   650

HERAKLES   Let me go to someone else,
    Admetos. Please. I ask it as a favor.

ADMETOS   Impossible.
    You must stay.

(to a servant)

                        —You there. Take our guest inside.
    Open up the guest rooms on the east wing
    of the house. Then serve him dinner and wine.
    Be generous. And shut the doors on the courtyard.
    I do not want our guest to be disturbed at dinner
    by the sounds of mourning.

                                    HERAKLES is escorted inside.

LEADER   . Are you mad, Admetos?
    Your wife not dead an hour, and you can bear the thought
    of entertaining guests?

ADMETOS   This man is my friend.
    What would your answer be if I turned my friend away   660
    from my home and city? That I deserved your admiration?

Surely not. And what would I gain?
My wife would still be dead.
My loss would be exactly what it is,
neither more nor less. But I would lose a friend.
I have pain enough without the pain
of having my house called inhospitable and rude.
I am his host; he is my friend and guest.
His hospitality to me is lavish, unsurpassed
in generosity and love, when I stay with him in Argos.   670
And Argos is a thirsty place.

LEADER   Your friend, you say.
Then why conceal your sorrow from your friend?

ADMETOS If he suspected what had happened here,
I do not think he would have stayed. Some, I know
will shake their heads and say that what I did
was wrong. But this house of mine has yet to learn
discourtesy to guests or less than due regard
for those with claims upon my honor and my love.

Exit ADMETOS into the palace.

CHORUS
Hospitality is here.
What house could be more gracious or more generous   680
than this? Open-handed, always prodigal and free,
its master gives such lavish welcoming
that one might think his guests were gods.
Great gods have sheltered here.
Here Apollo, god of Delphi, condescending,
came, his high divinity constrained to serve
as shepherd for a year. And down these blessèd hills,
to mating flocks the god of music sang the season's song,
O Hymen Hymenaios O!

So powerful Apollo's song   690
that spotted lynxes crouching in the mountain rocks

were drawn by joy, no longer wild, to stray like browsing sheep
beside the shepherd god. And here, compelled
from Orthrys' shaggy glens, the golden lions came.
Bright god, so sweet your clarity of song,
the fawn came shivering from the darkened wood,
and there, beside the forest edge, shyly stepping
from the arbor of the pines, the strong light caught her—
dappled, on delicate legs, dancing as Apollo sang:
O Hymen Hymenaios O!   700

Your guest was god, Admetos. And so,
by grace, your house is now beyond all mortal houses
blest in wealth of flocks beside the clear blue waters
of Boibias. Westward, mile on mile
across the greening plain, your tilth and pastures range
to far Molossos where the lord of light drops down
to ford his horses in the Adriatic night;
and eastward too your kingdom goes, across the peaks
where Pelion takes its headlong plunge, harborless and sheer,
down to the green Aegean. Admetos, all   710
this blessèd land is yours, by grace of god.

And now, again, this gracious man
has opened wide the doors and welcomed in this house
another guest. Another—even though the wife he loved
was newly dead, and the agony of grief
lay freshly on him . . . Noble man, his courtesy
and grace exceed all human scale. But who can say?
Greatness of soul is all that human wisdom knows;
all philosophy is in it. I stand in awe,
Admetos. And somehow I have faith, a growing hope   720
that for this noble, heaven-minded man,
all, by grace of god, may still be well.

                              Enter ADMETOS from the palace.

ADMETOS My friends, I appreciate your kindness and support.

Thank you for remaining. The funeral is ready now
and my men are bringing out the bier.

Enter Attendants slowly and solemnly, with the bier of
ALCESTIS *on their shoulders. Reverently, they set it down directly before the great central doors of the palace.*

But first,
before we take her body to the grave,
I would like you, friends, to speak the customary words:
the last farewell. We shall not see her in this life again.

LEADER Wait, Admetos.
I see your father Pheres on his way, and servants with him
bringing gifts to offer to the gods below.   730

Enter PHERES *dressed in mourning black. His shorn hair is
white and he is stooped with age; he walks slowly up the ramp
to the bier of* ALCESTIS; ADMETOS *faces him on the other side
of the bier.*

PHERES   Son,
I have come to help you bear the burden of your grief.
You have lost a good wife: a decent, loving,
humble wife. A hard and bitter loss, but bear it
you must.

*He motions to his servants to come forward
with the funeral gifts.*

Accept these tokens of my respect,
and let her take them with her to the world below.
We must honor her in death as she deserves;
she gave her life to let you keep the light. No,
she would not let this poor old man drag out
his dying years deprived of all he had—his one,   740
his only, son. And by her bravery in death,
she has been a credit—no, a glory—to her sex.

64

(*formally addressing the body on the bier*)

—Lady,
rest in peace.
By your courage you have been the savior of my son.
Your generosity restored the fortunes
of my broken house, when it was down. Alcestis,
fare you well, even in the world below.
And rest in peace.
                              —Mark my words, son.
Marriage is for most of us a losing proposition.
But this wife of yours was pure gold, and no mistake.
And gold is what I give her now.   750

He signals to his servants to lay their gifts upon the bier, while
                    ADMETOS *angrily steps forward to intercept them.*

ADMETOS Who asked you to come? Who invited you?
Not I. Not her.
Love? *What* love? Your love's a lie: all words.
So keep your gold. She'll never wear your trinket
love.
She'll be buried as she is. Without your gifts.
Or you. Leave. Who needs you anyway?
Who needs you *now*?
You came, you say, to bring me sympathy and help.
The time for you to help was when I had to die
or find a substitute. Where were you *then*?   760
Vanished. Nowhere. Like your love. You disappeared
and let another take your place in death.
You were old, and she was young.
And now you have the gall to come here with your mock
sorrow and your hypocrisy of love!
You never gave a damn for me!
Where was your love when I needed you? Why,
for all you cared, I might have been some slave's bastard
smuggled in the house and set to suckle at the breast
of that barren bitch who calls herself my mother.   770

No, when courage was required,
when dying was the issue and the test,
you showed us what you really are.
Not my father, but a cheap coward!
Gods, is there any coward in this world like you?
There you were, a withered bag of bones, tottering
into eternity. But still you wouldn't die! Not you.
You didn't dare to die. So you let a woman,
no blood of yours, do your duty for you.
To her and her alone I owe the tenderness and love   780
I would have lavished on my parents in their age,
had they loved me like a son.
If I were you,
I would have fought—yes, *fought!*—for the privilege
of dying for my son. Besides,
your time was short. A few brief years at best.
So what had you to lose?
Every happiness a man could have, you had.
You inherited a kingdom when you were still a boy.
You had a son, so your succession was secure   790
and you could die in peace, knowing there would be
no rival claimants for your throne, no wars.
You cannot say that you abandoned me
because of my neglect: I showed you all the honor
a son could give. I was always good to you
in your old age. And how have you repaid my love?
You would have let me die.
Well, now your time is running out, old man.
So hurry. Use what little time you've got to breed
another son to care for you in your old age and stuff you   800
in the ground.

(*raising his hand.*)

So help me gods,
I will never lift a hand to bury you!
You refused to lift a finger for my life.
I disown you both.

If I still live and see the light,
everything I might have owed to you as son,
I pledge to her who gave me life.

Gods, how I hate them,
all these aging hypocrites, tottering around,
telling you how much they want to die,   810
stuffed with self-pity, whining about old age
and its indignities, their long, slow, crawling passage
to the grave.
But let them get the slightest glimpse of Death
and suddenly they stick like leeches to the light
and tell you life is not so bad.

LEADER Stop it, both of you.
Haven't you sorrows enough without this too?
                                        Boy,
why must you exasperate your father?

PHERES Boy,
who in god's name do you think you are?   820
Are you my master now, and I some poor, bought,
cringing Asiatic slave that you dare dress me down
like this? I am a free man, Thessalian born,
a prince of Thessaly. And I will not be bullied
by the likes of you, arrogant boy.

                        ADMETOS *turns angrily away.*

                        Hear me out.
Don't think you'll pelt me, boy, with your abuse
and then just turn your back.

Damn you, boy,
I made you lord and master of this house of mine.
I gave you life, I raised you.

I am not obliged to die for you as well.   830
Or do you think my father died for me?
There is no law, no precedent, in Greece
that children have a claim upon their fathers' lives.
A man is born to happiness, or otherwise.
He is born for himself.
Everything you had the right to get from me, you got.
I made you ruler of a rich and populous country.
And I intend to leave you all the vast domain
my father left to me.   840
So how have I hurt you? What more do I owe you?
Life?
No. You live yours, and I'll live mine.
Do your own dying. I'll do mine.
You love the light.
What makes you think your father doesn't love it too?
The time we spend beneath the earth, I think, is very long.
And life is short, but what there is of it is good,
good and sweet.
                   As for fighting, boy, you fought all right.
You fought like hell to live—life at any price!—
beyond your destined time. You only live   850
because you took her life. You murdered her.
And you dare talk about my cowardice—
you, who let a woman outdo you in bravery,
let her give her life to keep her gigolo
alive?
But you're clever, I admit.
Immortality is yours, yours for the asking.
All you have to do is wheedle your latest wife
into dying in your place.
And then, like the cheap coward that you are,
you accuse the rest of us of failing in our duty!   860

ADMETOS Listen—

PHERES   You listen, boy. Remember this.
You love your life. Well, so does every man alive.

68

And if you call us names for *that*,
worse things will be said of you. They won't be pretty,
and they'll all be true.

LEADER There have been too many ugly words, too much abuse,
already.
            —Old man, stop provoking your son.

ADMETOS Let him talk, and then I'll have my say.
                                    —You see?
The truth hurts. Your cowardice was your mistake.
You didn't dare to die.   870

PHERES   That was no mistake.
The mistake would have been dying for you.

ADMETOS And dying young is just the same as dying old?

PHERES One life is all we have. Not two.

ADMETOS The way you clutch at that one life of yours,
you'll outlive Zeus.

PHERES   How have I hurt you
that you should hate me so?

ADMETOS   Old age
has made you greedy. Greedy to live!

PHERES Greedy, am I?
Who killed that girl whose corpse you're burying?
And you talk to me of greed!   880

ADMETOS It was your cowardice that killed her.

PHERES You took her life. You killed her.

ADMETOS O gods, I hope

I live to see the day when you come crawling to me
for help!

PHERES That's your style, not mine.
Find some woman to help you live. Marry *her*,
then let her die.

ADMETOS Your fault. You wouldn't die.

PHERES No, I wouldn't.
This god's light is sweet, I tell you, sweet.   890

ADMETOS You cheap coward, you don't deserve to live!

PHERES Go bury your dead.
Whether you like it or not, *I'm* still alive.
You won't gloat over my dead body. Not today,
boy.

ADMETOS Don't expect the world to praise you when you die—
if you ever do.

PHERES What the hell do I care what people say of me
after I'm dead?

ADMETOS Gods,
what shabby, shameless cowards these old men are!

PHERES *She* wasn't shabby, was she? No, she was *brave*.   900
Brave enough—stupid enough—to die for you.

ADMETOS Leave. Let me bury my dead.

PHERES I'm leaving.
Let the murderer bury his victim in peace.

Exit PHERES, *followed by his servants with the rejected gifts.*

ADMETOS Go and be damned to you,
           you and that woman I used to call my mother.
           You have no son.
           Grow old, both of you, as you deserve—
           childless, heirless, alone.
           Never let me see you in this house again.   910
           So help me god,
           if I had heralds here to proclaim
           that I disown you both and ban you from my house,
           I'd do it.

           A long silence ensues as PHERES *slowly makes his exit, and*
                ADMETOS' attendants take up their position by the bier.

           (*to* CHORUS)

           And now, friends, let us perform our sad task,
           and take Alcestis' body to the grave.

           The Attendants lift the bier of ALCESTIS *to their shoulders and
           the funeral cortège moves slowly and solemnly toward the
           right. Leading the procession is the bier, which is followed by
               ADMETOS and the children, and finally the entire CHORUS.*

LEADER Fare you well, Alcestis.
           Let Hermes of the unseen world receive his honored guest,
           and the Dark Lord welcome you below as your nobility and
                     love deserve.
           For if the good fare best, and courage has its due   920
           even in that pale democracy below,
           the Queen herself of all the dead will rise in homage,
           seeing you, Alcestis.
           No braver mortal ever lived.

           *Exeunt omnes in slow, funeral procession. For a while the
           stage is empty and silent. Then an old* SERVANT, *wearing a
           scowling mask, appears from the palace. He speaks directly
           to the audience. Now and then, as he speaks, the voice of*

71

> HERAKLES *can be heard singing, off-key and indistinctly, the*
> *snatches of a familiar drinking-song.*

SERVANT I've seen a lot of strangers in my time,
        guests traipsing in here from all over the world,
        and we put 'em all up, bed 'em, and feed 'em
        food. But this newest guest is the worst damned
        guest this house and I have ever seen. Right away,
        anyone could have seen Admetos was in mourning.   930
        So what does this dull clod do? Barges in,
        big as life and bold as brass. I mean,
        any man with a grain of decency or ordinary common sense
        would have seen Admetos was in trouble
        and accepted what we had to give without a lot of noise
        and fuss. But not this fellow. Nossirree,
        if we don't fetch him what he wants, he yells at us
        to shake a leg. "Hurry up!" he bellows. "Dammit. *Move!*"
        Then he picks up a great big wooden bowl of wine—
        both hands at once, just like a peasant—   940
        and swills it down, straight, unwatered, strong,
        and reddish black like the ground that grew it.
        Well, before you could say Dionysos,
        he was heated up, half-crocked, high
        as a kite. Then he slaps a wreath of myrtle on his head,
        and starts in murdering some bawdy song.
        Listen . . .

> *From within is heard the bray of a drunken voice, singing.*

        There *he* was, roaring away over his supper,
        without a thought for poor Admetos and his troubles,
        and there we were, mourning for our mistress,
        and what with the maids wailing and beating their breasts—   950
        well, you've never heard such a bloody medley in all
        your days. And of course we couldn't tell him we were mourning
        because king Admetos had given orders forbidding it.
        Anyway, here I am, left
        behind at home to entertain this so-called guest

(though, if you ask me, burglar or highwayman
or just plain pirate is closer to the mark).
And meanwhile they've taken our lady to the grave,
and I didn't get to follow her body or hold out my hand
and say goodbye to her the way I wanted.   960
Because she was good to us all, a good, kind mistress,
more like a mother than a mistress, always
calming the master down when he went off in one of his fits
of rage. Anyway, that's why I hate the sight
of this guest who came barging in on our troubles.   .
Guest or no guest, I detest the man
and, god knows, I've got the right to hate him.

Enter HERAKLES, *tipsy and reeling, from the palace. On his
head he wears a wreath of flowers; in one hand he carries a
flask of wine, in the other a large cup which he periodically
drains and refills. His speech is punctuated by periodic hic-
cups and emphatic belching.*

HERAKLES Hey, you there!
Yeah, I mean you, with the big frown on your face!
What'sh your problem, sourpuss?   970
Butler'sh oughtta be polite, goddamit.
Servish with a smile.
An' none of those goddam killjoy looksh either.
Here I am, your mashter's bes' fren',
an' all you can do is glower at me with that goddam
miserable mug. An' why?
'Cause someone you barely knew dropped dead.
Dead . . .
C'mere, fella,
an' I'll let you in on a l'il secret.
Make a better man of you.   980
I mean, wise up:
we all gotta die.
You know what it'sh like to be a *man*?
I mean,
d'you really unnerstan' the human condishun, fren'?

73

I can see you don't. How could you, with a face like that?
Well, lissen, mister:
we all gotta die. An' that's a fact.
There's not a man alive who knows the odds on death.
Here today. Gone tomorrow.
Poof.
That's fate. A mystery. I mean,   990
there's jus' no knowin'. Man can't figger it out.
Well,
that's my message. So what d'you say?
Cheer up and have a l'il drink,
huh?
Live for the day. Today is ours.
Tomorrow's fate.
Hey,
an' there's somethin' else, Yessir. Aphrodite.
Don't forget Aphrodite, fren'.
'Cause thass a good l'il goddess.
They just don' come any sweeter than Aphrodite.
Take my advice, fella, an' forget your troubles.   1000
Well, what d'you say?
Am I talkin' sense? Damn right I am.
So forget whatever it is thass makin' you so goddam
glum. Come on, man,
have a drink. Drown your troubles.
Here, put these flowers on your head,
and bottoms up!

He drains his glass and refills it.

Lissen:
you hear that wine purling and gurgling in the cup?
Well, a swallow of this will do wonders, friend,
for whatever's ailing you.   1010
I mean, we all gotta die. Right?
Well, that's why we all gotta think human thoughts,
and live while we can.
Eat, drink, and be merry.

Take it from me,
the way those gloomy, bellyachin' tragedians gripe,
life isn't life at all, it's just a goddam
funeral.

SERVANT Quite, sir. I understand.
But, sir, this happens to be a house of mourning.
Your drunken revelry is grossly out of place. 1020
Sir.

HERAKLES Izzat so?
Jus' because a woman's dead? Stranger too, I hear.
Sure, it's sad, but what's the tragedy? Look,
the family's alive and well.

SERVANT Alive and well?
You mean you still don't know what happened here?

HERAKLES Of course I know. Admetos told me when I came.

(pulling himself together, more soberly)

Wait.
Are you saying that Admetos lied to me?

SERVANT You know the master, sir. He is hospitable to a fault.
Sometimes his kindness goes too far.

HERAKLES I know his kindness well. 1030
Is that the reason I must go without my supper?
Because of some dead stranger?

SERVANT Stranger, you say?
Oh, sir, what stranger could ever be as close as she?

HERAKLES (soberly now, with genuine concern)
What has happened here?
What is Admetos hiding from me?

SERVANT   Sir, let it be.
          She belonged to us.
          Go, and let us mourn our dead in peace.

HERAKLES So it wasn't a stranger who died?

SERVANT   If it were,
          nobody would have minded your getting drunk.   1040

HERAKLES Then Admetos lied to me? Deceived his friend?

SERVANT   Sir, you couldn't have come at a worse time.
          This is a house of mourning. Our hair is shorn;
          we are dressed in black. You can see for yourself.

HERAKLES Who died, man?
          One of the children? Old Pheres? Who?

SERVANT   Admetos' queen, sir. Alcestis. Alcestis is dead.

HERAKLES Alcestis dead?
          And you were entertaining me when she lay dead?

SERVANT   Sir, Admetos honors you.   1050
          He could not bear the thought of turning you away.

HERAKLES What husband ever lost a wife like this?
          Oh, Alcestis, Alcestis . . .

SERVANT   When she died, sir,
          it seemed as though the whole house, every one of us,
          died with her.

HERAKLES Oh, I knew it, I knew it
          when I saw his face all red with weeping,
          and his hair shorn, and the bitter anguish in his eyes!
          And, like a bloody fool, I believed his story   1060
          that he was burying some stranger.

A stranger!
And then he made me enter, forced me to come in,
against my will, and accept the welcome of his house.
And then, while he was suffering, mourning his wife,
there I was, his dearest friend,
—gods!—
feasting and carousing like some stupid, drunken clod,
wreathing my head with these damned flowers!

> *He rips off his wreath and dashes it to the ground.*

And you let me do it!
The whole house was throbbing with this sorrow,   1070
and you never said a word!

Quick, man.
Where is the funeral being held?
Where can I find Admetos?

SERVANT Go straight that way, on the road to Larisa.
Just outside the walls, sir, you'll see the place,
a tomb of polished marble.

> *Exit into palace.*

HERAKLES Now, Herakles,
your great ordeal begins.
Come, o my tough spirit, you hard, enduring hands calloused
          with my many labors,
come and prove what man I am.
Prove me Herakles,   1080
the hero son my mortal mother bore to Zeus almighty!

Alcestis is dead,
and I must bring her back to the fields of light,
home, safe, to Admetos' arms, and so discharge my debt

of gratitude and love. Admetos' love to me was great,
and it deserves—and it will get—no ordinary kindness
in return.

Soon, I think,
the god of Death, those black wings beating overhead,
will come swooping down and settle by the grave
to drink the sacrificial blood. I'll lie in ambush   1090
there beside the tomb, and when the Dark Lord comes,
I'll break from hiding, seize him with my arms,
and clamp him in a hold so hard he cannot break it,
god though he is. Let him struggle.
I'll crush him in my mortal grip until he does my will
and lets Alcestis go.

But if Death fails to come,
if the blood stays there untasted on the ground,
I'll go beneath the earth, down to the unseen world
                below,
confront the god of Hell and his Persephone,   1100
and demand Alcestis back. Make no mistake:
I'll force my way below and bring Alcestis home,
and consign her to Admetos' care.
For he deserves this thanks from me:
His house was overwhelmed with grief,
but even so, he took me in, he made me welcome here.
Kind and noble to a fault, he hid his loss
to do me honor as a friend. Where in all Thessaly,
where in all the world, could I find a friend
as generous as this? I could not do it.   1110
And it will not be said of me
that this good and noble man conferred his kindness
                on a friend
unworthy of his love.

Exit HERAKLES *to stage right. There is a brief silence. Then the*

CHORUS *re-enter from the left, followed by the forlorn and*
grief-stricken ADMETOS.

ADMETOS O home no home
emptiness   silence   pain   loss
going in or coming out   O
walls of pain: I cannot leave   cannot stay
Hurt   has no words
Hurt   will not be still
O   1120
        let me die
better never have been born
I envy the dead   the dead are beautiful
not here my home
                        down   down
my home is with the dead
I hate the light   I hate this earth
O Earth, come over me
and let me die
so lovely is the hostage that I gave to Death
my life is all below

CHORUS (*individually, while* ADMETOS *sobs helplessly in response*)
—Take your grief inside, Admetos. Hide, hide   1130
from the light.
                —You have cause for grief.
—You have suffered, heaven knows.
—But grief will never bring her back.
—The truth is hard.
                —Accept it, Admetos:
—You will not see her in this life again.

ADMETOS Good friends, the wound is fresh,
and you have opened it again . . . Better,
better by far, it would have been
if we had never married, she and I, never loved,
never lived here in this house together!   1140
How I envy them, those men who never marry,

men who have no children, who live for themselves,
alone. Then each would have one life to live.
That pain would be his, nothing more.
He does not live to see his children sicken,
his wife dying in childbirth . . .
Who that had a heart to love would choose such pain
if he could live alone and never know
how much he had to lose?

CHORUS —It had to be. We cannot choose our fates.   1150
—A man can fight. But not with life,
   not with death. ·
                            —Accept it like a man.
—Hard, hard, I know.
                            —Be brave, Admetos.
—Courage. Others too have lost their wives.
—Some soon, some late, every man is curbed
   by suffering or fate.
                            —Now it is your turn.

ADMETOS This sorrow lasts forever. There is no end to pain
when those we love go into that eternal night
beneath the earth. Why, why, in the name of heaven,
friends, did you stop me when I tried to die   1160
with her? There, in one grave, she and I,
we could have been together always. Always.
And then the lord of Death would have us both,
two lives instead of one. Loyal in love,
we would have crossed that dead water together.

LEADER (with the utmost simplicity)
   Admetos, a friend of mine once lost his son, a fine young
boy of exceptional promise, and an only child. His father was
an old man, white with age, and in the last years of his life.
But he bore his loss with dignity, as bravely as he could.

ADMETOS This house, how can I call it home? How can I go in, remem-   1170
bering how happy I once was here, and how, of all that happi-

80

ness, nothing now is left? *Then* and *now:* a gulf so great it
seems two wholly different unconnected worlds. I remember
then. It was dusk on our wedding day. All around us the pine
torches were blazing, and she and I were coming home to bed,
escorted by a noisy crowd of happy friends and guests, singing
and dancing. I remember how they congratulated me, and
how they wished Alcestis happiness and long life (oh, my
dead Alcestis!). In our marriage, they told us, high nobilities
on either side had merged and met. And *now?* Now the only   1180
song is the cry of mourning. And the friends who bring me
home wear black instead of white. And the bed is there, the
bed is there . . . I sleep alone.

LEADER Your luck had been good, Admetos. High happiness and great
wealth—both were yours. So when this sorrow struck so suddenly, it found you unprepared. Suffering was something you
had never known.

　　　Still, your life is yours; you still have wealth. True, you have
lost your wife and the comfort of her love. So have other men.
Is it so strange, really, that human marriages should end in
this divorce of Death?

ADMETOS Dear friends,
　　　strange as it may seem,
　　　I think my wife in death is happier than I am now.
　　　No pain, no hurt, will touch her anymore.   1190
　　　She rests in peace, free at last from all
　　　the endless agony of life. And fame is hers
　　　forever.

　　　As for me,
　　　I should not be alive. I should be dead.
　　　The life I have is not worth living. I know it now.
　　　Too late.

　　　How can I bear to go on living in this house?
　　　What happiness is there in coming home, home to this
　　　　　　　dead house,

with its sound of absence, its echo of a voice
that greeted me when I came home? And now nothing, nothing
but this dead silence.   1200
When I go in, the emptiness inside will drive me out.
The empty rooms, the empty bed, the chair she used
to sit on, and the shining floor all dark with dust,
and the children sobbing, huddling at my knees
wherever I go, crying for their mother,
and the servants mourning their dead mistress,
remembering a gentle presence that my house has lost
forever . . .
                    I cannot stay here.
                                    But in the city
I will see my married friends, friends with wives;
the girls and women thronging to their festivals and
            dances . . .   1210
The very sight of it would drive me home. All
Alcestis' friends, the girls she used to know—
I could not *bear* to see them now. Not
now.

And I have enemies. Behind my back,
they'll point me out, whispering, "Look there,
look at Admetos,
the man who was afraid of death,
the coward who let his wife go down to Hades
in his place? Do you call *that* a man?
What kind of man would curse his father and mother   1220
because he was afraid of dying?
Who but a coward?"

Friends, you say my life is still mine.
But what's the good of living,
when everything I valued in this world is gone,
when I have lost my honor with my wife?

            He stands motionless, head down, in silent despair.

82

CHORUS Necessity is stone.
        Call her death, compulsion, fate: against
        what man her cruelty comes, that man is doomed.
        If poets know, if scholars speak the truth,   1230
        nothing stronger, nothing more resistless,
        is.
        O Man,
        against her hard, relentless coming on,
        all your craft and intellect are weak.
        There is no power in your spells and Orphic songs;
        no virtue in your herbs, your healing lore. Nothing,
        nothing can resist her coming on. Only patience.
        Suffer and submit.

        Necessity is stone,
        implacable. She has no face
        but rock; no human shape or likeness owns,   1240
        no cult, nor shrine. She heeds no sacrifice.
        She is force, and flint; no feeling has, no
        pity. None.

        (*kneeling, all together*)

        Mistress, Lady without mercy, I have felt
        your stroke before. May you never come again!
        Only by your hard strength the will of Zeus is done.
        By sheer force you break the iron of the Chalybes.
        Your will is granite, cruel. Nothing helps. Only patience.
        Suffer and submit.

                The CHORUS *now turn and address* ADMETOS *directly.*

        Admetos, now
        this goddess holds you in the bitter bondage of her grip.   1250
        Bear it. Be brave. Though you should mourn Alcestis always,
        you cannot bring the dead to life. Great heroes
        die. Even the sons of heaven fade, darkened

83

into death, though they were dear, dear as life
to the grieving gods. Alive, Alcestis had our love;
love will be her portion in the world below, for she was
brave. To her, Admetos, you were bound by bonds of love.
Then will you be less brave?

Glory is her right,
Admetos. Do not let Alcestis' grave be numbered   1260
among the ordinary dead. Make her grave a shrine;
honor it as men would honor gods—a holy place
beside the road where those who journey kneel and pray.
The traveler will see her grave and, turning off,
will say of her, "She gave her life to save another.
She is a blessèd spirit now, and so may also bless.
In homage men will kneel before her grave and pray:

(*all together, kneeling*)

"Hail, Lady, mistress of mercy, by your bravery and love,
bless us and be gracious."

Enter HERAKLES, *followed by a veiled girl.*

HERAKLES Admetos,
when a man is angry with his friend,   1270
he should speak his mind frankly and freely;
not keep his feelings smouldering inside.
As your friend, I thought I had the right
to stand beside you in your hour of need
and prove my loyalty.
But you misled me;
you deliberately concealed the truth:
instead of telling me that Alcestis was dead,
you let me think that you were burying a stranger.
Then you made me welcome in your unhappy house,   1280
you gave me food and drink, as though nothing
had happened here, nothing at all.

There you were, in mourning for your wife,
while I, like a clod, was wreathing my head with flowers,
pouring long libations to the happy gods, getting
drunk. *Drunk* at a time like this!
But how was I to know?
It was *wrong* of you, Admetos, wrong, I tell you,
to treat a friend this way. But let it pass.
You have sorrows enough, old friend.   1290

Listen: I have a reason for returning.

(*indicating the veiled girl standing behind him*)

You see this woman?
Do me a favor: Keep her here for me,
in your care, until I finish with my mission
in Thrace. I will come for her on my return,
after I have killed Diomedes, and captured his
                    horses.
But if I don't come back—Heaven avert the omen!—
then keep the girl as a servant in your house:
my gift to you. And no small gift, either.
This woman wasn't easily won, Admetos.   1300

ADMETOS Where did you win her, Herakles?

HERAKLES Not far from your house, I happened to pass by a place
          where athletic games were being held, contests
          open to all comers. And the prizes offered
          were very tempting. Well, in a word,
          I entered the contest and I won the prize—
          this woman here.
          The winners in the minor events won horses.
          But in boxing and wrestling the prizes were oxen—
          and they threw in the girl as a bonus.   1310
          Well, as luck would have it, there I was,
          and it seemed a shame to lose such splendid prizes.

85

So here she is. Now, as I said, Admetos,
I'd like you to keep her. Take care of her. She's worth it.
And she's not stolen either, if that's what you're thinking.
I won her fair and square in a damned hard fight.
Someday, Admetos, you may be glad I did.

ADMETOS Herakles,

my reason for concealing my wife's death from you
was neither disrespect nor any lack of love.
God knows,
I had troubles enough without driving you away   1320
to look for shelter somewhere else.
Alcestis' death is mine to mourn. Mine alone.
My sorrow is enough.

As for this woman here,
I beg you, my lord, if you can somehow manage it,
please, take her somewhere else.
Give her to some friend who is not in mourning.
Tell him to keep her. You have many friends in Pherai.
But please, please.
don't remind me of my loss. Seeing this woman here,   1330
here in Alcestis' house, day in, day out,
would be more, much more, than I could bear.
I am crushed with sorrow as it is, Herakles.
Do not burden me with more.

Besides,
where in this house could a young girl stay?
I mean, she *is* young. I can see it, Herakles,
in her jewelry, in the style of clothes she wears.
How could she live here, surrounded by young men?
How could I protect her? Young men are lusty,
their desires not easily controlled.   1340
                                        —Herakles,
it is you, your interests, I am thinking of.

What can I do? Put her in Alcestis' room?
Take her to Alcestis' bed?
I can hear the gossip now, people in the city
saying I ran to some other woman's bed,
and betrayed the wife who died to save me.
Worse, I can hear Alcestis' voice, reproaching me
from underground. And where Alcestis is concerned,
I cannot be too scrupulous. She and she alone
deserves my love. ·   1350

(*turning to the veiled woman*)

                    —Woman, whoever you are,
I tell you this, you look like my Alcestis,
so much like her: the same figure, the same height . . .
You are beautiful too . . .

                                        He hides his head.

Herakles,
for god's sake, take this woman away,
out of my sight! I am weak now, do not make my weakness
                    worse . . .
Oh, looking at this girl, I seem to see
my lost Alcestis . . . And my heart starts churning,
and the tears—

                                        He sobs unashamedly.

O gods, gods in heaven,
now, now, for the first time, I know the anguish of my life . . .   1360

LEADER   Sorrow: there is nothing more to say.
It does not matter who or what we are.
The gods do with us what they will. We must bear it.

HERAKLES   If only I had the strength, Admetos, to bring your wife
back from the world below, back to the light,
I would have done it.

ADMETOS   I know. But why speak of it?
The dead are dead. They never come back.
Never . . .

HERAKLES   Control yourself. Bear it like a man.

ADMETOS Bear it like a man? Easier said than done, Herakles.

HERAKLES Suppose you mourned her all your life, Admetos?   1370
What good would it do?

ADMETOS   No good at all.
I mourn because I must. I loved her . . .

HERAKLES I know:
Nothing hurts like losing those we love.

ADMETOS I lost myself when I lost her. Lost myself—
and so much more.

HERAKLES She was a beautiful woman, worthy of your love.

ADMETOS I loved her so much I do not want to live.

HERAKLES Your loss is still fresh. Time will dull the pain.

ADMETOS If time is death. Death will dull it.

HERAKLES A new wife, a new bride, will help you to forget,   1380
Admetos.

ADMETOS Silence, Herakles. Not another word.
How could you suggest such a thing?

HERAKLES   You won't remarry?
No woman, ever?

ADMETOS No woman will ever share my bed again.

HERAKLES Alcestis is dead. How does this help her?

ADMETOS Wherever Alcestis is, she deserves my honor.
          I owe it to her.

HERAKLES   And I respect your feelings.
          There are some, of course, who would call you foolish.

ADMETOS Let them call me anything they want.
          Anything but bridegroom.   1390

HERAKLES   I admire you, Admetos.
          You are loyal in love.

ADMETOS She is dead.
          But I would rather die than betray her love!

HERAKLES Nobly spoken, my good Admetos.
                                        Well, then,

          (taking the veiled girl by the hand and bringing her forward)

          make this woman welcome in your generous house.

ADMETOS By your father Zeus,
          I beg you, please, no! Anything but that.

HERAKLES You will be making a mistake, if you say No.

ADMETOS I would never forgive myself, if I said Yes.

HERAKLES Obey, Admetos.   1400
          Let me have my way. The courtesy you show this girl
          may serve you in your time of need.

ADMETOS   O gods,
          how I wish you'd never won her in those games of yours!

89

HERAKLES Friends share and share alike.
          When I am winner, you are winner too, Admetos.

ADMETOS   Splendid, Herakles.
          Then make this woman leave. Immediately.

HERAKLES If she must. But *look* at her first, Admetos.
          See if she should go.

ADMETOS   (*not looking*)   She *must* go.
          You won't be angry with me, will you, Herakles?

HERAKLES I have my reasons for insisting, Admetos.   1410

ADMETOS   I surrender. You win.
          But I disapprove. Your insistence displeases me.

HERAKLES You may forgive me soon. Humor me for now.

ADMETOS   If I must, I must.

          (*to Attendants*)

                         —Servants, take this woman inside.

HERAKLES Slaves?
          No, I will not surrender this girl to slaves.

ADMETOS   Then take her in yourself.

HERAKLES   No, she is yours,
          Admetos. I will not give this woman to anyone but you.

ADMETOS   And I refuse to touch that woman's hand.
          Let her go inside by herself.

HERAKLES (*taking* ADMETOS *by the right arm*)
                              No, Admetos.

I have faith in your right hand—and yours alone.

ADMETOS (*unsuccessfully attempting to withdraw his arm from*
       HERAKLES' *grip*)
       My lord,
       I protest: you are forcing me against my wish.

HERAKLES Courage, Admetos. Welcome your guest.
       Here, reach out your hand. Now take her hand
       in yours.

           ADMETOS (*reluctantly stretching out his hand, but carefully
           averting his face*)
                Here is my hand.

HERAKLES   Good gods, man,
       the way you act you'd think she were some Gorgon
       to turn you to stone.

       (*gently and ceremoniously, he joins the hands of* ADMETOS *and*
                ALCESTIS)

       You have her?

ADMETOS   I do.

HERAKLES   Then keep her, Admetos.
       She is yours, to have and to hold.
       Someday, Admetos,
       you will know your kindness was not wasted
       on the son of Zeus, your good friend and grateful guest.   1430

                        He raises ALCESTIS' *veil.*

       Now, Admetos, look. Look at her.
       Doesn't she look a little like your own lost Alcestis?

                        ADMETOS *stares in silent disbelief.*

Rejoice, old friend.
Be happy. Your day of mourning is over.

ADMETOS   O god, gods in heaven!
This is some miracle I see, impossible, incredible!
Oh, is it you? You, Alcestis? Is it really you?
Or is this just some mockery, some sweet illusion
sent me by the gods?

HERAKLES   No mockery, Admetos,   1440
but your own wife, in flesh and blood, your own
lost Alcestis!

ADMETOS   How do I know this is not some ghost from underground?

HERAKLES   I am your friend, Admetos,
not some vulgar trafficker in sorcery and ghosts.

ADMETOS   But I buried her today . . . How can this be?
Is it really Alcestis?

HERAKLES   The very same Alcestis.
I am not surprised you find it strange.

ADMETOS   Can I touch her? Speak to her?
Can she breathe? Does she feel and hear?

HERAKLES   Speak to her, Admetos.   1450
You have what you wanted. You have it all.
Take it.

ADMETOS   Alcestis!   O Alcestis
eyes I love   o sweetest face
these dear hands I never thought to hold again!
You are mine   so incredibly   mine
again   again!

HERAKLES   Again, Admetos. And may no jealous god envy you
your happiness.

ADMETOS   O my noblest, kindest friend!
                  Dear son of great Zeus, may Heaven bless you.
                  May the great god who fathered you guard you
                  and keep you safe, as you saved me,   1460
                  you alone, and gave me back my life.

                  But tell me:
                  how did you bring Alcestis back to the light?

HERAKLES I fought with the god who had her in his power.

ADMETOS Death!
                  Where did you find the god?

HERAKLES   Beside the grave.
                  I took him by surprise, then threw him to the ground.

ADMETOS Ah.
                  But why is Alcestis so still? Why can't she speak?

HERAKLES Until three days have passed,
                  and the bitter stain of death has disappeared,
                  she is forbidden to speak.   1470

                  Now, Admetos, take her in.
                  And in the future treat your guests and those you love
                  as they deserve.

                  And so, goodbye.
                  My master Eurystheus is waiting in Argos,
                  and I have labors to perform.

ADMETOS Stay with us, Herakles. My house is yours.

HERAKLES Another time, Admetos.
                  I have work to do. Work that cannot wait.

93

ADMETOS Success go with you, friend.   1480
But when your work is done, come back and be
our guest.

Exit HERAKLES.

—To all my subjects and fellow citizens,
I here and now proclaim a feast of thanks and praise
to celebrate the happiness of this great event.
Let the high altars blaze and smoke with sacrifice.
From this day forth we must remake our lives,
and make them better than they were before.

Happiness is mine, and now I know it.

Exit ADMETOS, *with* ALCESTIS, *into the palace*

CHORUS The gods have many forms.
The gods bring many things   1490
to their accomplishment.
And what was most expected
has not been accomplished.
But god has found his way
for what no man expected.
So ends the play.

Exeunt omnes.

94

NOTES ON THE TEXT
GLOSSARY

NOTES ON THE TEXT

A NOTE ON THE STRUCTURE AND PRODUCTION OF GREEK DRAMA

Greek plays are not, like modern plays, divided into a given number of acts. Their effective structural unit is the *episode*, which contains everything lying between the choral lyrics (*stasima*). The *prologue* contains not only the initial expository speech but all the action prior to the entrance of the Chorus. The first choral song is called the *parodos* (from the "entrance" of the Chorus). A *monody* is the lyric song (sometimes recitative) of a single character; the lyric exchange between a character and the Chorus is called a *kommos*. The last episode, called the *exodos* (from the "exit" of the Chorus), contains everything after the final *stasimon*. There was no fixed or even customary number of episodes and *stasima*. Characteristic of ancient drama, and especially of Euripides, is the *agon*, a carefully structured (often schematically elaborated and counterpointed) confrontation between characters, frequently of an adversary nature. (Examples of the *agon* in *Alcestis* are the delicate "deathbed" exchange between Alcestis and Admetos and the angry debate between Admetos and his father Pheres.)

It is important for the modern reader to remember that Greek drama was a *masked* drama, and that the masks not only "distanced" both characters and action but mediated the character's condition and psychology and even the "generic" quality of the action. In the vast space of the Greek theater, masks—supported by costume, stylized gesture, and metrical and rhetorical conventions—made it possible for the dramatist, at one blow, to identify his characters and "place" them—in their condition, age, and sex—vis-à-vis one another. If we can trust ancient (though late) sources, the masks were devices of "modal" inflection, means of stating the crucial generic facts. Thus a "sallow" mask indicated that its wearer was "in love or unfortunate"; other masks—masks with squalid features, matted or disheveled hair—indicated extreme suffering or derangement; an old man was instantly identified by his white beard, a youth or ephebe by his beardlessness, etc. Women's headgear (coifs, fillets, etc.), adornment, clothing (cf. *Alcestic*, l. 1337) indicated whether the wearer was young or old, rich or poor, married or unmarried. By these means the age, condition, and sex of a character were at all times theatrically *visible*. This generic visibility is crucial, since it both excludes intimate naturalism and imposes a *generic* account of human existence. This generic account, we should note, is quite compatible with a rich, complex psychology; the psychology, however, is not individualistic, but generic and even metaphysical. Since intimate expression and gesture—winks, nods, frowns, "body language" —were not theatrically visible, they had to be indicated verbally, by means of dramatic speech. The language and diction of Greek drama are, of course, highly rhetorical (as well as incredibly rich in metrical and syntactical nuance), and this rhetoric is designed to support the masking convention both by reinforcing its generic aspirations *and* also compensating for the loss of expressive means imposed by it. For this reason—its uncolloquial "elevation" and its complexity of nuance and metrical complexity—it is the despair of translators. We simply do not possess the apposite modern poetics.

A word of caution. Too much has been said, especially in theatrical handbooks, of the "hieratic" qualities of Greek drama. Elevated it clearly was; but priestly and hieratic, surely not. Increasingly, scholars now regard the familiar notion of Greek drama—with its stiff, "ritualistic" mannikins, its high shoes, and grimacing Halloween masks—as a stereotype based, not on fifth-century, but Hellenistic and Graeco-Roman, theatrical practice. As far as can be ascertained, fifth-century actors did not wear high buskins, grotesque masks, or stiffly ornate clothing. That is, fifth-century practice, though clearly "elevated" by modern or even Elizabethan standards, was based upon a dignified— but essentially representational—realism. As so often, the practice of the "great age" is distorted by the reverence accorded it by epigones, and this reverence is then passed on as an authentic account of "classical" practice.

Finally, the modern reader should constantly bear in mind the immense complexity of Greek drama—a complexity that sharply differentiates it from almost any other drama we know of. He should remember, for instance, that Greek drama is, in terms of its metrics, quite incredibly subtle, supple, and rich (and, further, that these subtleties were evidently appreciated by an audience whose aural sophistication, wholly ear-trained, must have been astonishing). We should also remember that these metrics are constantly involved with dance movements (of which, unfortunately, we know almost nothing); and, further, that these dances were visual embodiments of feelings which, precisely because *kinetically* embodied, could reinforce words and also move *beyond* the words and so express what words could not. To dance we must *also* add the presumably crucial—but irreparably lost—dimension of music. If we cannot even imagine now what this music sounded like, we should at least be aware that Greek drama tends—increasingly, as the fifth century drew to a close—toward the condition of music; that, in a very real sense, this was *operatic* drama. Moreover, if Euripidean practice can be taken as representative, music, like dance, was used not as a decorative addition to language, but to express what language could not. We can tolerate quite incredible silliness in a libretto or an aria simply because the music, in the hands of a great composer, transcends the words it pretends to mediate; becomes, as we like to say, pure feeling. We shall never know what Greek drama was like at the ultimate verge of feelings, at the point (cf. the Note on the stage direction following l. 503) when words fail altogether; but we should never *read* a monody or choral lyric or *kommos* without remembering that these pieces were written to be *sung*. We should also perhaps remember that they were sung, not only by the actor, but later, after the performance, by the audiences who heard them (like those Athenian sailors who, according to tradition, spent the night before a dreaded battle, singing songs from Euripides' *Andromeda*); in short, that Greek drama was not a Mandarin drama but, like Shakespeare or nineteenth-century Italian opera, one of the few truly great popular art forms the world has ever known.

1-116 *Prologue*

1-16 *Apollo's prologue.* I have deliberately pointed up and expanded Apollo's language here, and the literal-minded reader may reasonably wish to know why.

If I am right in my view of the play, Apollo's language and condition here (a god *compelled* to be a *slave*) are meant to be starkly contrasted with the case of Admetos (a *mortal* man *exempted* from *death*). The contrasting is, I believe, too vivid and schematic to be anything but deliberate. In large part the vividness of the contrasting depends upon our understanding that, to the Greek mind, god is defined as a being that does not suffer; man, in contrast, is a suffering thing. Here, for effect, Euripides deliberately reverses the common situation: Apollo is the "suffering servant," Admetos the "deathless mortal." The apparent paradox is of course a device of emphasis.

The contrasting here is essentially a contrast *a fortiori*; the man and the god, so different in powers and condition, define each other in opposed weakness and strength, doom and exemption. Such contrasting is commonplace in Greek literature, as we should expect; in an aristocratic culture, the weak are instructed, exampled, in their modalities and fates, by those stronger than themselves. In the *Iliad* Achilles tries to accept his own death by arguing that "even Herakles"—a stronger hero than Achilles—had to die; later, Achilles urges his victim Lykaon to accept *his death* without fuss because better men than Lykaon have died. To a Greek audience such modal contrasts were, I believe, accepted easily and naturally. Moderns still employ—and can still respond to—moral argument *a fortiori*, but it is hardly second nature. Tolstoy's Ivan Ilych, for instance, convinces himself of his mortality, not by the power of example, but by the force of a syllogism: "Caius is a man, men are mortal, therefore . . ."

Unless verbally stressed and pointed up, this kind of contrast is apt to be lost in a modern dramatic performance. Not only is it unfamiliar, but, in performance, we cannot, as in a poem or a novel, return to the words; they must do their work *now* or not at all. And in a play like this —a modal play, I would argue, which appropriately begins with a violent modal contrast—the emphasis seemed to me too important to be lost to worries about excessively "interpretative" translation. The evidence is *there*, in the actual language, in the shaping of the thought. We will *hear* it, in the Greek, in the unmistakable humiliation and indignation of Apollo; in the constant language of service, compulsion, doom, endurance: "I endured [*etlēn*] . . . although a god [*theos per ōn*] . . . a serf's table [*thēssan trapedzan*] . . . for Zeus compelled [*ēnangkasen*] me . . . to serve a mortal man [*thēteuein . . . thnētoi*]. . . ."

And, if we hear it, we are likelier to hear the obsessive modal language of the play elsewhere, and to note the recurrent modal contrasting, all designed to throw Admetos' crucial exemption into the sharpest relief.

7-8 *The author of my shame was Zeus. He killed/ my son Asklepios . . .* According to Pindar (*Pyth.* 3), Asklepios had offended Zeus by restoring the dead to life, thereby threatening the gods' prerogative of immortality. In the thematic structure of the play, Asklepios' "conquest of death" provides a parallel to Herakles' contest with Death and, ultimately, to Alcestis' *aretē* in confronting Death by dying for her husband.

23 *I outwitted the Fates.* By getting them drunk, according to Aeschylus (*Eum.*, ll. 723 ff.).

60 *Don't be afraid, Death.* The ironic note is unmistakable, and typically Euripidean. So too is the abrupt transition from Death's appropriately portentous style to Apollo's delicate banter and sophistic legalisms. The director who wants to produce Euripides must be prepared to cope with a dramatic master who, like Chekhov, delights in mixing modes usually kept distinct, in flickering, lambent irony, in transparent parody; who constantly crosses tragedy with comedy, and undercuts his own solemnity with self-mockery. And nowhere is this pleasure more in evidence than in this play.

83 *the younger my victim.* The preference of Death for a younger victim is a common motif of folklore. Underlying this belief (and the ritual of human sacrifice) is the conviction in primitive agricultural communities that the Earth (which includes the spirits of the dead and "the old ones") can only be fertilized by the blood of the living. The Earth is thought of as a womb which is quickened or renewed by the spermatic action of blood. The younger and fresher the blood, the more potent its fertilizing effect, as can be glimpsed in an Aztec poem on a feast of human sacrifice: "The youth chosen was of radiant countenance/ of good understanding/ quick and clean of body/ slender like a reed . . ./ He who was chosen was entirely without defect" (William Brandon, *The Magic World, American Indian Songs and Poems*, pp. 15 ff). So too, in Euripides' *Hecuba*, Achilles' ghost cannot be laid until it receives fresh blood; and it characteristically wants the vigorous blood of the young Polyxena, not that of old Hecuba. Indeed, the persistent theme of *youthful* sacrifice in Euripides rests not only upon the notorious idealism of the young but upon the refusal of the chthonic powers to be appeased by anything less vital. Hence Death here regards it as detrimental to his honor (*geras*) that Alcestis' death should be deferred until she is old; and Death is in this respect an aristocrat of the old school, quite untempted by the mercenary bribe of the plutocratic Apollo. (We may assume that Death would have grumbled had Admetos' mother or father offered to make the supreme sacrifice.)

In later times, with the progress of morality and the eclipse of the old chthonic religion, the human sacrifice became, it would seem, first a crippled or deformed victim, and finally an animal. In modern times Death himself has been eclipsed and his office transferred to (old) politicians. See, for instance, John Peale Bishop's "And When the Net was Unwound Venus Was Found Ravelled with Mars":

This was in the time of the long war
when the old deliberated and always rose
to the same decision: More of the young
must die.

117-190 *Parodos.*

147 *where is the cleansing water* . . .   In a house of mourning it was customary to set a basin of pure spring-water at the door so that visitors could, when leaving, purify themselves from the pollution of death. Presumably for the same reason Apollo must leave Admetos' house, lest his divinity be "stained" by death.

150 Custom also prescribed that mourners should place a lock of their hair on the tomb of the departed (as in the recognition-scene in Aeschylus' *Choephoroe*, ll. 167 ff.). The present passage is the only one indicating that it was also the practice to dedicate a lock of hair in the house of the deceased.

166-8 *at holy Ammon's/ healing touch, the dying desert makes/ a miracle of green.* The Greek gives merely "at the waterless shrine of Ammon." Expansion is required to make the underlying religious and pictorial sense effectively vivid. The great oracular shrine of the Egyptian god Amen-Ra (Ammon) lay in the Libyan desert at the oasis of Siwah. W. S. Hadley cites what is probably an early Baedeker account of the place: "Siwah is a little paradise: round the dark blue mirror of its lakes there are luxurious palm-woods, and orchards full of oranges, figs and olives." To a traveler approaching the shrine from the bleak, waterless desert, the green oasis must have seemed the miraculous revelation of a life-giving god—the very image, to despairing eyes, of sudden life and hope. A Greek audience would have known about the site and work of the shrine either from the Greek inhabitants of Cyrenaica or the temple attendants in (Greek) Thebes, where Ammon had a statue and a cult.

180 *death-tamed and -broken men.*   My effort to get the sense of the Greek phrase *dmathentas* (literally, those who have been "tamed" or "subdued," a metaphor or euphemism for "the dead"). The name "Admetos," as

noted in the Introduction, means "the untamed one"—i.e. the man exempted from death. (Cf. Bacchylides, fr. 47 Ed., who, speaking of the gods, says that they are, unlike men, "untamed," "unbroken," by cruel diseases.) So too, at l. 1247, the Chorus says that Necessity "tames" or "breaks" (*damadzei*) the iron of the Chalybes.

194-287 First episode.

208-9 *She will be buried as we knew her . . . a queen.* Literally: "The adorn-ments (*kosmos*) are ready in which her husband will bury her." *Kosmos* means both "beauty" and "adornment" (i.e. funeral adornments, the expensive gold-stitched robes, jewelry, perfumes, etc. customarily buried with the dead). It is the idea of beauty *and* costliness that makes the Leader exclaim, literally: "Let her know then that she dies with all glory . . .". The custom of burying the dead in golden splendor caused ancient legislators to pass laws against excessive funeral expenditure—the ancient equivalent of "conspicuous consumption." Both in ancient times and now, *kosmos* was, to the Greek mind, very much the concern of the living. In 19th-century Smyrna the traveler A. W. Kinglake observed, "A Greek woman wears her whole fortune upon her person, in the shape of jewels, or gold coin . . . enabling a suitor to *reckon*, as well as to admire, the objects of his affection" (*Eothen*, ch. v).

226 *"Bright goddess who guards my home . . .* That is, Hestia, goddess and in-carnation of the domestic hearth.

288-324 First *stasimon.*

313 ALCESTIS, *supported by* ADMETOS *. . .* It is of course impossible to ascertain the appearance of Admetos and Alcestis: their clothing, masks, etc. But they should not, for want of consideration, be allowed to fade into that indeterminate life reserved for the characters of a theater whose acting conventions and traditions have not survived and can only be conjec-turally restored. The director who confronts the task of staging the *Alcestis* simply cannot avoid making a decision; and it would be better for him and for audiences alike if scholars could be trained to *visualize* performance.

Can we, in fact, visualize Admetos and Alcestis? What kinds of masks did they wear? How old are they? In a modal theater—i.e. a theater based upon the generic—such questions are crucial. It makes, for instance, all the difference in the world whether we see Antigone as a young woman or (as I believe) a very young girl; the age of Pentheus very seriously affects our understanding of the *Bacchae*. Obviously certainty is impossible, but there are reasonably strong hints.

Alcestis, for instance, seems to be young, quite young. Admetos at line 1336 calls her *nea* (young); and, although she has two small children, it is also true that Greek girls, especially of noble family, married early, around the age of fourteen. That is, Alcestis may be no older than eighteen or nineteen; she would be, in that case, the "young matron." Admetos, I believe, is also young. Pheres (at line 843) ironically calls him a *kalos neanias* (i.e. "handsome youth"—with a sarcastic suggestion of ephebic beauty), and one can reasonably ask how such description could have been meaningfully applied unless it tallied with the mask and appearance. Admetos is twice called "boy" (*pais*), by the Chorus in remonstrance, and by Pheres in scorn. There may also be visual evidence of actual repertory practice. In portraying scenes from Greek drama, 4th-century Apulian vase painters, according to T. B. L. Webster, probably conveyed the general ideas and outlines of a repertory practice. Thus in the earliest extant portrayal of the play, on an Apulian *loutrophoros* of the late 4th century, we see, standing beside a buxom, seated Alcestis, the sorrowful figure of Admetos, depicted as a handsome and *beardless* young man. (For illustration and comment, see A. D. Trendall and T. B. L. Webster, *Illustrations of Greek Drama*, London, 1971, p. 75.) Finally, there is the suggestive fact of Admetos' general inexperience (the Chorus at line 1183 call him *apeirokakos*, "inexperienced in suffering")—an inexperience that in Greek thought is insistently associated with youth and that, in my opinion, mediates the portrayal of Admetos throughout the play.

312-529 Second *episode*.

325 ff. *O Sun/ Sweet shining light . . .* Alcestis' words here are in lyric meters and spoken (or sung) with the poetic intensity of the dying. Admetos, in sharp contrast, responds in the more banal iambics of dialogue. Later (l. 365), as he begins to realize what he is losing, he too will turn to lyric anapests and a new level of intensity. Ultimately, in the *kommos* (ll. 1114-1269), when he finally and fully comprehends his own anguish, there will be no mistaking the intensity of his language and feelings.

367-8 *by your love we pray you/ live.* An effort to get the full sense of the concentrated (but quite elusive) Greek. Literally, Admetos says, "For we reverence [*seboumetha*] your love [*philian*]." While it is true, as Dale points out, that *sebein* need not mean "to revere or worship [as a god]," the utter dependence stated by Admetos in the previous line ("in you we live in you we die") suggests that the strong (i.e. worshipful) sense of *sebein* is being employed here. And this seems in part vindicated by the Chorus' recognition of Alcestis as a "blessèd spirit" (*makaira daimōn*) at line 1266.

375 ff. *Admetos, I am dying.* The abrupt tonal shift from the intensity of Alcestis' lyrics to this comparatively controlled and reasoned death-bed dialogue with Admetos, is understandably disconcerting to modern readers (and directors) of Greek plays. We can only say, with Dale, that Greek tragedy, and Euripides in particular, has "many scenes where a situation is realized first in its lyric, then in its iambic aspect, that is to say, first emotionally, then in its reasoned form." This alternation of lyric and reasoned dimensions—as though we were shown *seriatim* the facets of the situation—must be regarded as a convention which, however difficult it may be for moderns to accept, apparently did not trouble ancient audiences.

503 ff. *Sobbing and crying, the children throw themselves . . .* At this point in the Greek text there is a monody assigned to Alcestis' little boy, Eumelos. I have excised this song in its entirety, not because the passage is spurious or doubtful, but because, to modern taste, and, without music, it is intolerably maudlin. For those readers who might wish to know the words actually *sung* by little Eumelos, I offer the following literal rendering:

Alas for my fate! Mother has gone below. She is no longer in the light, Father. She has left me, poor woman, and orphaned my life. Look, look to her eyelids, at her arms hanging limp. Listen to me, Mother, listen. It is I, Mother, who call to you—your little fledgling, pressing my lips to yours. I am young, Father, left alone and forsaken by my dear mother. I have suffered pitifully, and you, dear, sister, have suffered with me. Ah, Father, your marriage was all in vain. You failed to reach the goal of old age with her. She died before you died. Now, Mother, with your going away, our house has been destroyed.

Euripides' purpose in this monody is clearly pathos, a musical resolution designed to stress the final poignance of Alcestis' death, as well as its impact upon Admetos' whole house. Pathos of this kind and degree, we must assume, was emotionally satisfying to Greek audiences. Athenian juries, for instance, expected, and evidently enjoyed, highly pathetic appeals from defendants; indeed, plaintiffs often capped their formal defenses by bringing into court their wives and children, sobbing and wailing, in order to work upon the feelings of the jurors.

Here, unmistakably, ancient and modern taste diverge. It is revealing, for instance, to compare Eumelos' baroque grief with a terse and tight-lipped sequence in Kurosawa's great film *Ikiru*. The camera shows us a car in which a small boy and his father are following a black hearse; the hearse holds the body of the boy's mother. As the hearse suddenly turns a corner, momentarily disappearing, the boy says, solemnly and matter-of-factly, "Daddy, Mother's leaving us behind." Elliptic and low-keyed, this is presumably as much as modern audiences are prepared to tolerate in the ticklish genre of childish grief (as opposed, say, to sentiment in romantic love, where Greek taste was positively chaste and severe in comparison).

Readers should also bear in mind that Eumelos' monody, like all monodies, was meant to be *sung*; and that in these monodies Greek drama is much closer to Italian opera than to Shakespeare or poetic drama. Given good music and virtuosity in the singer, Eumelos could have overcome the limitations of his actual words as easily as Handel's Julius Caesar succeeds in overcoming the feeble libretto and the absurdity of a castrated *imperator*. Indeed, one has merely to transcribe Eumelos' words into conventional operatic Italian (*Ahimé, il mio crudel destin! . . . Giovin son' o padre mio, sconsolato ed abbandonato*", etc.) to realize that the words are in fact librettist's Greek; that they belong essentially to music and are effective *only* insofar as their expression is finally musical. To poetry they have no pretension.

530-568 Second *stasimon*.

530 ff. *Farewell, Alcestis.* My translation of this lovely ode is admittedly "interpretative," designed to point up the enabling conceit and the poetic implications of details the Greekless reader could not be expected to glean from a literal translation. Thus I have stressed what I believe to be the central poetic figure of the ode—the bright image of Alcestis, whom Death would have "extinguished" in the sunless world of Hades, but whose aretē, in its deathlessness, cannot be eclipsed; then, again, in the second strophe, Alcestis merges with the moon which, like Alcestis, carries through the darkness the recurrent reflection of the sun's "light." Such stress may seem to some a trespass against the reader's rights: a tendentious turning. But I am concerned less with readers here than with audiences—audiences who cannot for obvious

reasons be expected to cope with conventions which, because unfamiliar, tend to be elusive, especially in "theatrical time." The choral dances and the music which presumably mediated the meaning of the words are gone, and the translator must, if he can, compensate for their loss. There is, in any case, no lack of literal versions of the ode; the dissatisfied reader is invited to consult one of those.

The three notes immediately following are designed to demonstrate to the skeptical that the strategies adopted here are considered, even meditated, techniques.

532-3 *those on whom the sweet light never shines: unseeing/ and unseen.* An example of translation by expansion or intruded gloss. Literally, the Greek reads: "May you be happy in the sunless house, in the halls of Hades." The modern reader without Greek is unlikely to know that Hades was commonly derived from the word meaning "unseen" (*a-idēs*). The dead are those who do not "see the light" (the common idiom for "life"); and when the living die, they are extinguished in every sense: neither seeing nor seen. That this play on the meaning of Hades is present in the ode is confirmed not only by the persistent light imagery, but by the word "sunless" in apposition with "Hades." None of this word-play, so crucial to our understanding of the ode, is visible in a literal version; to relegate such explanations to footnotes and commentary seems, at least in this case, a counsel of pointless despair.

533 *We shall not see your like again.* This line is my own contribution, but it is not, I think, gratuitous, since it is implied in the *valedictory* quality of the preceding lines—a quality conveyed by a rich conventional language of valediction—a language quite lost to us.

534 *O Death, in that dark tangle of your mind . . .* An effort, obviously conjectural and risky, to *think* my way *beneath* the poet's description of Hades here as "black-haired" (*melangchaitas*). Clearly, the epithet reinforces the etymological meaning of Hades (see Note on ll. 532-3), but it also seemed to advance the conceit. Hades (or Death), it struck me was "black-haired" not only because of his dusky kingdom, but because of the apparent obscurity, to men, of his purpose. Why, after all, *should* Alcestis die? Since the point of the ode as a whole, and of this sentence in particular, is to "cry defiance to Death," it seems appropriate that the Chorus should ask Hades, bent on his obscure purpose, to *recognize* the distinction and (shining) *aretē* of Alcestis. The "dark

tangle" of Death's mind is, I should confess, the *trouvaille*, uprooted from a very different context, of a great English religious writer.

569-678 Third *episode*.

571 *Obligation, friend.* I have rearranged in order to get the sense of "compulsion" at which the dramatist is aiming. Literally, the Chorus ask Herakles, "To what wandering are you *yoked?*" (The yoke, in Greek drama, is a persistent image or metaphor of necessity.) There is no way of conveying this is English without clumsiness or muting the point ("Where are you *bound?*" conveys the proper sense, but the metaphorical sense of "bound" is dead). For this reason I have transferred the statement of necessity to Herakles' reply.

As in the opening speech of Apollo, so here too Euripides moves swiftly to strike the important, thematic note. Like Apollo, and despite the paternity of Zeus and his great physical strength, Herakles is *bound* to a life of *labor* and toil for a *master*, Eurystheus of Tiryns.

600-1 *Rough, uphill/ all the way.* The depiction of Herakles' life as one of arduous, patient struggle and obstinate fortitude (tlēmosynē) is a commonplace of classical myth and art. On the metopes of the great temple of Zeus at Olympia, Herakles' labors were portrayed as a parable of the ordeals imposed upon civilized (and civilizing) men. Plato speaks admiringly of the (5th cent.) sophist Prodikos because he had presented Herakles as the hero who had chosen the arduous "road" of moral action as opposed to a life of pleasure and ease.

622 *Both. Both. I am in agony, Herakles . . .* With characteristic economy, Euripides makes Admetos' deception of Herakles here do double duty. Not only does he persuade Herakles to accept hospitality in a house of mourning, but in the process of deception we see him already acting out, *exploring,* the remorse and loss he is beginning to feel. His own loss is vivid enough that it brings him, for the first time, face to face with the transcience and "dreamlike" quality of human existence; death and life seem to converge. So too he anticipates his own later discovery that, in Alcestis' death, he lost his own life.

636 *Was she related to you?* Herakles' question and Admetos' answer provide a good example of Euripides' skill in achieving emotional tension and economy by means of ambiguity. Asked whether the dead woman was related (sungenēs) or a stranger (othneios), Admetos answers that she was a stranger, but then, quickly and equivocally, adds, "But she was connected (*anankaia*) with my house." The noun *ananke* (of which *anankaia* is the adjectival form) means, in fifth-century usage, both "necessity" and "kinship." (The ambiguity is not accidental, of course; "kinship," because it expresses a *natural bond*, and because the language of social organization precedes philosophical language, is presumably the root-meaning; cf. Latin *necessetudo*, which exhibits the same ambiguity. Durkheimians would not be surprised.) Thus while ostensibly deceiving Herakles, Admetos reveals, through dramatic irony, his own, fresh awareness of his dependence upon Alcestis: the anguish of his newly found *need*. Admetos, we realize, is beginning to speak the language of necessity—to "think mortal thoughts."

651-2 *Impossible/ You must stay.* The overbearing quality of Admetos' language should be stressed. A few lines earlier Admetos exhibited a new awareness; now, confronted by a problem touching his honor as host—i.e. with traditional *noblesse oblige*—he begins to talk in the imperious, overbearing way of a man who has never known a check upon his will; who (unlike Herakles) commands but does not obey. In the finale Herakles will, in a spirit of strict (but friendly) "poetic" justice, overbearingly impose upon Admetos the duty of hospitality to a new "guest," the veiled woman who is Alcestis.

Modal psychology can be, I am convinced, no less complex and sophisticated than modern individual psychology. Here, in Admetos' veering between two metaphysical attitudes, between the new mortal knowledge of 626-7 and the old mortal ignorance shown here, we have a modal version of what would now be called "simultaneously conflicting attitudes." Medea's famous soliloquy in which she debates with (and within) herself whether she should kill her children is often hailed as a psychological novelty; but it is only novel because scholars think they see in it the advent of our psychology. In point of fact, the psychology involved is at least as old as Homer, but its antiquity should not blind us to the sophistication of Euripides' application, the *individual* genius with which an old psychology is here inflected and employed.

671-722 Third *stasimon*.

671 *And Argos is a thirsty place.* "Thirsty Argos"—thirsty because the land was parched and often drought-stricken—is an epic usage. Given Herakles' fondness for wine, especially in this play, it may not be amiss to sug-

gest, as I have, that Herakles' "thirsty Argos" was more related to Dionysos than Demeter.

679 ff. *Hospitality is here* . . . My strategy with this lovely ode is less radical than in the first *stasimon* (see note on ll. 530 ff.). Here and there I have heightened, but in order to provide the links and stresses that, in my opinion, any likely modern audience would require. The scale of Admetos' hospitality—imposed in part by timeless aristocratic practice —may be accessible to us as a kind of grand-seigneurial *largesse* (though *le grand seigneur* is hardly a flourishing species). We are much less familiar with the notion of houses (and hosts) that have gods as their gardeners, and even less familiar with the religious implications of such arrangements. In its final stanza, this Chorus express their fear of, and their admiration for, Admetos' magnificently excessive hospitality (as does the Servant at l. 1028). But *structurally* this hospitality is, in this ode, profoundly linked to the fact that a man, Admetos, had a god for guest (and servant); and also that Apollo's presence *blessed* the land, enriching its fertility and, indeed, imposing upon the countryside a kind of Saturnalia in which predator and prey, wild and civil, man and nature, are miraculously reconciled. The god's presence also affects Admetos by conferring upon him the attributes of the gods: happiness, wealth, deathlessness (or deferrable mortality); and we see these divine effects in the hospitality (as well as the lordliness and "high" generosity) of the prospering Admetos. To the Greeks, such prosperity was enviable but also dangerous, since heaven is jealous of human happiness. Hence the ambivalence of the Chorus here; they fear for Admetos' excessiveness, but recognize in it the exaggeration of a *noble* trait and the *explicit* favor of heaven.

703-4 *the clear blue waters/ of Boibias.* Both now and in ancient times, Boibias (or Boibeis) was a stagnant body of water. The conventional epithet *kallinaon* ("clear-flowing," "limpid") here applied to it has troubled commentators for obvious reasons. But the point is surely not some vague "poetic effect," but the miraculous results of Apollo's presence: marshes become limpid lakes, lynx and lamb lie down together, etc.

718 *Greatness of soul* . . . An attempt to render the quite untranslatable Greek word *aidōs*. In its full range *aidōs* means "self-respect," "respect for others," and, ultimately, "compassion." The man of *aidōs* respects, as we would say, "the rights" of others. But *aidōs* is essentially an aristocratic virtue; the man of *aidōs* is usually a man from whom, because he

is powerful and wealthy (as well as noble), the weak (e.g. the suppliant) can claim compassion; the guest, hospitality; the oppressed, protection, etc. It is because he is a man of aidōs—scrupulously and proudly so—that Admetos is so insistent that Herakles should accept his hospitality—and so vulnerable later to Herakles' insistence that Admetos should accept the "veiled girl," even though he knows that the likely result will be a violation of the aidōs he owes to Alcestis. "Greatness of soul" seemed to me to have the necessary "openness," as well as to provide a link to the aristocratic "greatness" that is its common prerequisite.

719 *all philosophy is in it.* The Greek word is *sophia*. Only partly intellectual in content, it is also an aristocratic virtue and suggests fineness of feeling or perception, broadening at its widest into the *skill* of mortality, especially compassion. "Philosophy" may be too intellectual and perhaps even anachronistic; but it has, except perhaps in academic circles, the necessary breadth.

723-1226 Fourth *episode* and *kommos* (1114-1187).

730 ff. Enter PHERES dressed in mourning black. I have transferred to the stage direction the Leader's description of Pheres' entrance: "with aged gait." In the Greek theater, even an old man's halting gait would have been hard to see; accordingly the dramatist obligingly writes the stage direction into the text.

The solemnity of Pheres' appearance—still another of those painterly groupings for which Euripides was famous in antiquity—should be stressed. Through the funereal dignity of Pheres' entrance, Euripides enhances the indecorousness of the subsequent "scene" between father and son. The purpose is not to shock, but to emphasize, through violence, the content of Pheres' words and, ultimately, to reveal, by contrast, the heroic dignity of Alcestis.

The ceremonial gifts would have included such things as gold or silver mirrors, vials of perfume, and other articles of a noble lady's toilette deemed useful in "the life below."

748 *Marriage is for most of us a losing proposition.* Mercenary and tactless, especially after Pheres' expression of "sorrow," these words are designed to be jarring. The translator may mute the effect to suit the modern taste for a single, smoothly modulated texture, but it seems a mistake to distort the dramatist's intent. In the Greek, Pheres' words are as unex-

pected as they are mercenary. And their very coarseness gives some tincture of provocation to Admetos' violent reply.

Modern readers should realize that Euripides' delineation of Pheres seems based upon a standard classical phenomenology of old age. Pheres, that is, is typical; *generically* old. In his *Rhetoric* (2, 12-13), Aristotle gives an account of the old which comes uncannily close to Euripides' portrayal of Pheres: "They are mean-spirited, because they have been humbled by life . . . They are not generous . . . and they are cowardly . . . and they are fond of life, especially in their declining years, since desire is directed toward what is missing and men particularly want what they do not have. And they are unduly selfish, for this too is meanness of spirit. And they live, not for the noble, but the expedient, and more than they should, because they are selfish. And they are more inclined to shamelessness than the opposite . . . for they pay little attention to what people think . . . ."

751-816 By any ancient standards, Admetos' speech here is shockingly violent. But its violence is largely a function of the Greek audience's strong sense of filial piety and respect for age. Admetos' anger reaches its peak when, at line 802, he says he will not assist at Pheres' funeral. Athenian law stipulated that even a father who had prostituted his son was legally entitled to be buried by that son; since Admetos' case against Pheres is less grievous, the refusal is meant to be outrageous.

There is also violence in Admetos' language. Thus we have constant anacolouthon, the choppiness of structure indicative of strong feeling, and the "abrupt asyndeton of rising passion" (Dale). The function of this verbal violence is not sensationalism or the prospect of "an interesting conflict between two egotists," but a careful effort by the dramatist to confront the audience with the conflict in its own values: on one hand, its actual (contemporary) values; on the other, the "ideal" values embodied in myth (as a residue of older cultural values). Through violence in language and structure, Euripides' tactic is to compel his audience to consider critically the quality of Admetos' traditional, mythical "heroism." He therefore hits precisely at the point—filial piety—where the audience's own operative values can be effectively enlisted *against* Admetos. Obviously doubts created by Admetos' conduct toward Pheres must tend to create doubts about Admetos' treatment of Alcestis (a subject on which both the received version of the myth and the "chauvinism" of the Greek male audience were either silent or complacent). Certainly the *dramatic* effect of Pheres' vigorous denunciation of Admetos' selfishness is to make it possible for the audience to see Admetos' conduct and Alcestis' sacrifice with fresh eyes.

In order to compensate for the absence of modern audiences of anything remotely resembling Greek *pietas* and respect for the old, I have heightened the violence of Admetos' words. What we cannot experience as an outrage to our values (because we lack the values which might be outraged) must be experienced as an affront to decorum and taste—"aesthetically," as we like to say.

768-70 The text is somewhat doubtful, but Admetos' point is clearly that Pheres was lacking in paternal love. He manages, ironically, thereby to raise doubts about his own legitimacy and nobility. The irony is less grotesque if the reader is aware that, for a Greek woman, the failure to produce children was grounds for divorce; hence it seems to have been fairly common for a barren woman to foist off a slave's child as her own. (cf. Aristophanes, *Thesmophoriazousae*, ll. 502 ff. and Euripides, *Phoenissae*, ll. 31 ff.).

789 *You inherited a kingdom when you were still a boy.* Since almost all of Admetos' charges against Pheres ultimately rebound on Admetos, one may wonder why he taunts Pheres with this particular piece of good fortune. The likeliest explanation, I suggest, is that Admetos had himself experienced the same good fortune. If so, it would be an additional hint of Admetos' youth. In the *Bacchae*, again, old Kadmos voluntarily abdicates the throne to his young grandson, Pentheus.

854 *her gigolo.* The phrase is admittedly strong, coarser than the Greek. Pheres is scornfully suggesting that Alcestis was infatuated with the sheer physical beauty of her "handsome young lover" (*kalou . . . neaniou*). A more accurate rendering perhaps would have been "your little Romeo" (or "Lothario"); but moderns are intolerant of anachronisms which Euripides and his audience would have accepted without qualms. Pheres' insinuations may be coarse, but their coarseness is Euripides' means of giving Pheres' words the gritty realism that his character and the situation require.

897-8 *What the hell do I care what people say of me/ after I'm dead?* By 5th-century standards and the implicit values of the *Alcestis*, these are ignoble words: no man of *aretē* could have uttered them. In a very real sense Alcestis regains the light because her *aretē* makes her, at least in terms of the human memory embodied in myth and literature, immortal. Pheres' words here are, in their baseness, an obvious foil to

Alcestis' nobility. But Euripides' revelation of Pheres' baseness, we should note, is carefully delayed until *after* Pheres has demolished Admetos' claims to *arete*. In this way the two male antagonists, father and son, are allowed to damage each other, with the result that Alcestis— against all male expectation—emerges as the sole surviving victor of this *agon*. For this reason, I think, Euripides concludes the scene with a brief funeral dirge in which the Chorus praises Alcestis' heroic endurance (*schetlia*), her patient bravery (*tolmes*), nobility and generosity (*gennaia*), and her *arete* (*meg' ariste*).

904 ff. Deletion of lines from a Greek play requires extreme caution. Right or wrong, I have deleted three lines from Pheres' speech here as probable interpolations, though they are metrically and lexically correct (as educated interpolations usually are). The reader may wish to judge for himself, however. In the text, Pheres goes on to say: "But you will be brought to book by her [Alcestis'] kinsmen./ If Akastos is still a man of courage, / he will avenge his sister's death." In my judgment, the threat of Akastos' vengeance is gratuitous, the kind of tidying up of minor details commonly exhibited by pedants, but rarely by great dramatists. A revenge-motif would be at odds with Euripides' clear *dramatic* interest in having Admetos recognize his own selfishness and guilt. Finally, the lines seem an intolerable interruption of the arc of rising violence, so visible in Pheres' words at line 881 and the matching violence of Admetos' reply.

984 ff. Enter HERAKLES, tipsy and reeling . . . My translation of Herakles' famous "drunken speech" may raise eyebrows among those who expect dignity and decorum from their Greek tragedians (if not always from Herakles). But Herakles's drunkenness here (tipsiness is a euphemism) is a dramatic *fact*, and too important a fact to be played down. Certainly there is no point in translating as though Herakles had taken one sherry too many and was beginning to "unwind." In details of diction but especially in its sentiments, the speech is unmistakably spoken by a drunken Herakles; if Herakles were not in fact drunk, his acute embarrassment later would be unmotivated. I have translated accordingly. Admittedly, Herakles' Greek is more correct and "sober" than my translation; but I assume that ancient dramaturgical conventions were in this respect different from ours. The ancient tragedian wrote his words and left it to the actor to inflect them; modern conventions—designed for a reading audience—tend to be rather more explicit.

1086 *and it will get* . . . The phrase is an intruded gloss, designed to sharpen, for the Greekless reader, what an ancient audience would have understood without being told—that is, the aristocratic punctilio involved in Herakles' promise here to restore Alcestis to Admetos. Aristocratic *aretē* is always competitive, and Herakles is determined not to be *outdone* by his friend and rival (in *aretē*), Admetos. If Admetos has treated Herakles with the hospitality one might give a god (and thereby failed to treat him with candor as a friend), Herakles in return proposes to respond with an even grander and more "godlike" gesture. The entire last scene clearly illustrates Herakles' friendly and aristocratic determination to force upon Admetos the same extravagant generosity (and also humiliation) that Admetos had earlier imposed upon him.

1088 *those black wings beating overhead* . . . The MSS. reading here is *melampeplon* ("black-garbed"), but the scholiast's comment makes it clear that *his* text read "black-wingèd." This seems appropriate since it echoes Alcestis' image of "wingèd" Death at line 350. But the point goes deeper than poetic detail. Throughout the play Euripides stresses the parallelism between Alcestis and Herakles; they share the courage (*tlēmosynē*) required to confront Death—Death in person. (For the same reason I would suppose that Death's wings should be *seen* beating with agitation in the *agon* with Apollo.)

1147-52 *Take your grief inside, Admetos* . . . In the Greek, each of these choral lines is followed by a cry of anguish (*aiai e e, pheu pheu*, etc.) from Admetos. Since modern English possesses no such stylized language of grief, translation is impossible. But the reader who doubts the sincerity of Admetos' grief should be aware that here and at 1129 ff. Admetos, in ancient performance, was reduced to inarticulate cries of grief (hence the efforts of the Chorus to rally him from excessive mourning).

1166-1187 *Admetos, a friend of mine once lost his son* . . . In the Greek, these lines are lyrical. I have resorted to prose for two reasons. First, it seemed to me important to vary a *kommos* which, without music, cannot be sustained as poetry for a stretch of nearly seventy-five lines. Second, the words spoken by the Leader at 1166 are, at least in sentiment, in their anecdotal simplicity, extremely unusual in Greek drama. In English they simply *work* better in simple, cadenced prose than as formal poetry. Once begun, such a style cannot be simply abandoned, so I have made Admetos answer in a similar vein.

1227-55 Fourth *stasimon.*

1227 ff. *Necessity is stone . . .* The culmination, in reflective, almost philosophical, choral song of the play's crucial language of constraint and the corresponding themes of human suffering and endurance (*tlēmosynē*) and courage (*aretē*). "Necessity" (*anankē*) is in some real sense a learned word; originally borrowed from ordinary usage, it would seem to have been applied by pre-Socratics and early sophists to phenomena—e.g. scientific causality—felt to be somehow at odds with older and more religious concepts of Fate. My translation deliberately skirts and occludes the highly self-conscious Euripidean beginning. (Literally: "I have lived with the Muses and I have soared into lofty regions and explored many learned writings, but I have discovered nothing stronger than Necessity. . . .") Euripides' beginning is self-conscious, I think, because he is aware of the risks of introducing legislated (and possibly controversial) "intellectual" language into a work presented to a popular audience. His own modernity and honesty forbid him to use a concept which, like the older word for Fate, Moira, was freighted with unwanted or obsolete religious meaning.

And though he speaks of Moira earlier in the play, he seems anxious here to subsume or bypass the older word in the more neutral and impersonal *Anankē*. For *his* purposes what mattered, I believe, is that the Chorus should express, in a striking and comprehensive way, the essential feel of the Euripidean universe: a world dominated by the operation of relentless "laws"; the loom of an ultimate Force, beyond the power of the gods themselves to change (even Zeus, according to the Chorus, must harmonize *his* will with Necessity); a Force wholly, incomprehensibly, removed from human concerns, and utterly indifferent to them as well. The gods—and perhaps dramatists—may delay or modestly obstruct the operation of this relentless and irresistible Force; but they do not in any real way affect its workings. Only against the looming of such a Force do human love, endurance, and courage become what they are here, in the close of this ode, the saving mortal skills of tragic (and also comic) survival. I do not expect all readers (or scholars) will agree with my conviction. But it is mine, and the ode, and the play, have been translated accordingly.

1253-4 *Even the sons of heaven fade, darkened/ into death . . .* The Greek for "darkened" is *skotioi*, a word which explicitly picks up the imagery of light and darkness that clusters around Alcestis' death and descent to Hades (where, the metaphors suggest, even Hades cannot eclipse the bright glory of her courage). See notes on 530, 532-3, and 534. The suggestion of the scholiast on this line, with its suggestion that we are meant to understand *skotioi paides* as equivalent to "bastard sons of heaven" should be, I think, firmly rejected.

Euripides, I should perhaps add, *does* compare Anankē to a sheer crag or cliff where compassion has no purchase. But the phrase "Necessity is stone," which begins the first two stanzas, is my effort to move directly to the key word and to do so in a way conducive to a feeling of formal statement. In the same way and for the same reason I have tried to resolve the first two stanzas with the terse iteration of the Chorus' later advice to Admetos: "Be patient./Suffer and submit." Lacking music and the metrical wealth and precision available to the ancient poet, I could see no other way of making these strophes work as poetry.

1269 Enter HERAKLES. I have omitted as theatrically clumsy (at least in modern production) the Leader's two lines announcing Herakles' return. Literally: "Admetos, here, I think, comes Alkmene's son on his way to your hearth." The size of the Greek theater may require such "cue" lines, but in this case the lines, I think, come from the poet's need to modulate between the preceding lyrics and the resumption of the dialogue.

1270-1488 *Exodos.*

1427 *You have her?* We have here, it has been held—persuasively, I think—a deliberate echo, indeed a parody, of the ceremony of betrothal (enguē, literally a giving of one's hand in pledge or troth). According to the formula, the bride's father (or nymphagogue perhaps) places the bride's hand in the groom's, then asks the groom, as here, echeis? ("Do you take her?"). The groom replies, as here, echō ("I take her hand"), and the father responds: soidze nun ("then keep it"). The parody is of course aimed directly, with gentle malice, at Admetos' promise earlier never to take another woman (or wife) into his house.

1444 *not some vulgar trafficker in sorcery and ghosts.* Words designed to lay to rest the audience's fear—frighteningly real in the 5th century—of ghosts and the underworld. Alcestis, Euripides assures us, is not some bloodless revenant from Hades; so too Admetos' house is only metaphorically Hades (insofar as Admetos' life has become a "living hell").Unless explicitly dealt with, the spectator's fear might jeopardize the wit and delicacy of the finale as well as Euripides' serious dramatic purpose here. Shakespeare in *The Winter's Tale*, a play tantalizingly close to *Alcestis* in mood and beauty, for similar reasons warns his audience, through Paulina, that the "miraculous" resurrection of Hermione has not been accomplished by devilish arts:

> I'll make the statue move indeed, descend
> And take you by the hand: but then you'll think,
> Which I protest against, I am assisted
> By wicked powers . . .

1472-3 *treat your guests and those you love/ as they deserve.* A key passage, whose translation is crucial to interpretation. Literally, Herakles says: "For the future, Admetos, be just [*dikaios*] and act with reverence [*eusebei*] toward strangers and guest-friends [*xenous*]." To my mind, the words are playfully, and importantly, ambiguous and "open." The injunction to "be just" we should understand in the usual classical sense, i.e. distributively: to treat others according to their *just merits*, to assign others their true *value*. The injunction would have little meaning if Admetos, by treating his *xenous* with *indiscriminate* regard (and also disregard), had not violated the spirit of *dikē*. The word *xenos* is of course ambiguous—and nowhere more so than in this play—ranging from "stranger" (as "enemy") to "guest" and thence "friend" and, finally, to anyone bound by claims of friendship or love (a sense nearly synonymous with *philos*). At line 1423 Herakles bids Admetos, ironically, to take the hand of the veiled girl (*xenēs*), who is both stranger and guest but also wife (earlier in the play Admetos claims that his house does not know how to reject or dishonor its *xenous*—though Admetos clearly dishonors the dead Alcestis when he welcomes his guest Herakles to his house). At line 1444 Herakles assures Admetos that, as *xenos* (i.e. as friend and guest), he is incapable of vulgar necromancy. By line 1472, thanks to these progressive inflections, the word can be applied to *both* Herakles and Alcestis (my translation "those you love" is designed so that it can include the application to Alcestis, as "friend" would not). Herakles, I am saying, is delicately (but also forcefully, in a world where delicacies of language and refined behavior were still understood) telling Admetos to discard his old grand-seigneurial habit of hospitality à l'outrance and to discriminate according to value and worth. Similarly, in the same spirit of true *human* justice, the Duke, in Shakespeare's *Measure for Measure*, advises the erring (but redeemable) Angelo:

> Well, Angelo, your evil quits you well.
> Look that you love your wife; her worth worth yours.

1489 *The gods have many forms* . . . Modern readers, accustomed to stress the concluding lines of a play, should perhaps be aware that this brief coda also concludes the *Bacchae*, *Helen*, *Andromache*, and *Medea*. Admittedly, the sentiment seems strikingly appropriate here; but it would be unwise to press a stylized exit-song for profound meanings.

GLOSSARY

ACHERON, one of the many rivers of Hades.

ADMETOS, son of Pheres, husband of Alcestis, and king of Thessaly.

AEGEAN, the sea lying between mainland Greece and Asia Minor.

AKASTOS, son of Pelias and king of Iolkos; brother of Alcestis.

ALCESTIS, wife of Admetos and daughter of Pelias.

ALKMENE, mortal woman who became by Zeus the mother of the hero Herakles.

AMMON, the Egyptian god Amen-Ra, equated by the Greeks with Zeus. His shrine, located at the oasis of Siwa in the Libyan desert, was the seat of a great oracular shrine.

APHRODITE, goddess of sexual love.

APOLLO, god of prophecy, healing, lyric poetry, and discursive (or forensic) speech. As god of light, he is distinct from Helios, the god of the sun. By the mortal woman Koronis he became the father of Asklepios, the "blameless physician" slain by Zeus. In Lykia (q.v.) his oracle at Patara was almost as renowned as the great oracle at Delphi.

ARES, the Greek god of war, and father of a fabulous horde of warlike sons.

ARGOS, city in southern Greece, frequently used to designate the region around it, and even to include the whole of the Peloponnesos. The western part of Argos was arid and so the country was proverbially called "thirsty"—an epithet in the translation playfully transferred to the hard-drinking Argives.

ASKLEPIOS, son of Apollo by Koronis, and culture-hero of medicine and the healing arts generally. For his *hybris* in restoring men to life by his simples and herbs, Zeus blasted him with lightning.

BISTONES, a wild Thracian tribe ruled by Diomedes.

BOIBIAS, a lake in Thessaly, at whose southern shore Pherai (q.v.) was situated.

CHALYBES, an Asian tribe, renowned in antiquity for their metallurgical skill and the hardness of the iron they worked.

CHARON, ferryman of the dead.

CYCLOPS (pl. Cyclopes) the one-eyed (or "wheel-eyed") smiths of Zeus who forged his thunderbolts. In Euripides' version of the myth, they were killed by Apollo for providing the thunderbolts with which Zeus killed Apollo's son Asklepios (q.v.).

DIOMEDES, legendary king of the tribe of the Bistones in Thrace, and son of the war-god Ares. Famed for his hatred of strangers, he was the owner of a four-horse team of man-eating horses. He died in combat with Herakles.

ELEKTRYON, son of Perseus and father of Alkmene; grandfather of Herakles.

EPIRUS, a territory of ancient Greece, bounded to the north by Illyria and Macedon, to the east by Thessaly, and the Adriatic (or Ionian) Sea on the west.

EUMELOS, son of Admetos and Alcestis.

EURYSTHEUS, king of Tiryns in Argos, who imposed upon Herakles the canonical twelve labors for which that hero was famous.

FATES, or the Moirai, conceived of as three spinning sisters. According to legend, Apollo outwitted the Fates and procured the deferment of Admetos' death by the simple stratagem of getting them drunk.

HADES, lord of the underworld, frequently equated with his own kingdom. (Etymologically, his name means "unseen," and his realm is therefore the home of the unseen, and unseeing, dead; the sunless kingdom.)

HERAKLES, son of Zeus by the mortal woman Alkmene, and the most renowned of all Greek heroes. Indentured to Eurystheus, king of Tiryns in Argos, he was compelled to undertake the twelve labors and the life of struggle and toil against the bestial and the barbarous, which made him the supreme culture-hero of the Hellenic world.

HERMES, god of heralds, travelers, thieves, etc. It was his function to escort the dead to the lower world. By stretching strings across the hollow shell of a tortoise from Mt. Kyllene, he became the inventor of the first lyre.

IOLKOS, a town in Thessaly at the foot of Mt. Pelion, and birthplace of Alcestis.

KARNEIA, a yearly festival of Apollo (Karneios) celebrated at Sparta and elsewhere during the period of the full moon in August.

KERBEROS, the fabulous three-headed dog who guarded the gates of Hades.

KORE, daughter of the goddess Demeter and, as Persephone, wife of Hades and goddess of the underworld.

KYKNOS, son of Ares slain by Herakles.

KYLLENE, a mountain in the Peloponnesos, site of the birth of Hermes.

KYPRIS, KYPRIAN, epithet of the goddess Aphrodite, who was reputed to have been born from the sea off the island of Cyprus.

LARISA, LARISSA, a town of Thessaly.

LYDIAN, of Lydia, a region of western Asia Minor, and a plentiful source of slaves for the Greek market.

LYKAON, son of Ares, god of war. He challenged Herakles to single combat and was killed.

LYKIA, a region situated on the southern coast of Asia Minor.

MOLOSSIANS, a Greek tribe of Epirus, here regarded as a part of Admetos' kingdom of Thessaly.

ORPHEUS, poet and musician of myth and legend who was reputed to charm trees, rocks, and wild animals by the beauty of his music. In religious cult his followers were the originators of a mystery of salvation, whose precepts were inscribed on sacred wooden tablets. For the purposes of this play he is, like Asklepios and Herakles, a saving culture-hero whose life becomes exemplary through confrontation with death. According to myth, he descended to Hades in order to bring back his dead wife, Eurydike.

ORTHRYS, a mountain about thirty-five miles south of Pherai.

PAIAN, a god of healing, frequently associated (and sometimes identified) with Apollo.

PELIAS, king of Iolkos and father of Alcestis.

PELION, a high mountain range in eastern Thessaly, sloping abruptly down to the Aegean Sea.

PERSEUS, Greek hero, ancestor of Alkmene and Herakles.

PHERAI, a town in Thessaly, situated to the southeast of the Pelasgian plain and the chief city of Admetos' kingdom.

PHERES, the father of Admetos.

PHOIBOS ("Bright," "Shining"), epithet of Apollo.

PHRYGIAN, of Phrygia, a country in the interior of Asia Minor, like Lydia a rich source of slaves for the Greek market.

PYTHIAN, pertaining to Pythia, the shrine of Apollo at Delphi.

SPARTA, chief city of the southern part of the Peloponnesos, site in ancient times of a cult of Alcestis.

STHENELOS, father of Eurystheus.

THESSALY, one of the largest regions of Greece, extending to Macedon in the north, the Aegean in the east, Epirus in the west, and Orthrys (q.v.) to the south. The Thessalian plain was famous for its good grazing and fertility, and Thessalians generally were praised for their horses and flocks.

THRACE, the vast region lying between Macedon and the Danube, bound on the south by the Aegean and the Sea of Marmara. In the early period it was regarded by Greeks as the wildest and most barbarous part of the world, and therefore peculiarly associated with the war-god Ares.

TIRYNS, one of the chief cities of ancient Argos, famed for its legendary association with Herakles. At the time of Herakles' labors, its king was Eurystheus.

ZEUS, chief god of the Greek pantheon.

At once a vigorous translation of one of Euripides' most subtle and witty plays and a wholly fresh interpretation, this rendition shows for the first time the extraordinary formal beauty and thematic concentration of the *Alcestis*.

William Arrowsmith, a distinguished classical scholar and translator and General Editor of the highly praised *The Greek Tragedy in New Translations* series, rejects the standard view of the *Alcestis* as essentially a psychological study of the egotist Admetos and his naive but devoted wife. He bases his translation on the conviction that this play, in keeping with Greek tragedy generally, is a drama of human existence, whose characters, while recognizably human and real, are also masked embodiments of human conditions. The *Alcestis* thus becomes a metaphysical tragicomedy in which Admetos, whose life heretofore has been exempt from all limitations, learns to "think mortal thoughts." He acquires that knowledge of limits—the acceptance of death as well as the duty to live, the knowledge of *how* to live *and* die—which, in Euripides, makes people meaningfully human, capable of both courage and compassion.